HEAVEN
That Better Country

HEAVEN
That Better Country

by
Jonathan Weaver, D.D.
Bishop of the Church of the United Brethren in Christ

"But now they desire a better country, that is, an heavenly."

"He looked for a city which hath no foundations, whose builder and maker is God."

"Here have we no continuing city, but we seek one to come."

SCHMUL PUBLISHING COMPANY
NICHOLASVILLE, KENTUCKY

Copyright © 2018 by Schmul Publishing Co.
All rights reserved. No part of this publication may be reproduced or used in any form or by any means—graphic, electronic, or mechanical, including photocopying, recording, taping, or information storage or retrieval systems—without prior written permission of the publishers.

Churches and other noncommercial interests may reproduce portions of this book without prior written permission of the publisher, provided such quotations are not offered for sale—or other compensation in any form—whether alone or as part of another publication, and provided that the text does not exceed 500 words or five percent of the entire book, whichever is less, and does not include material quoted from another publisher. When reproducing text from this book, the following credit line must be included: "From *Heaven: That Better Country* by Jonathan Weaver, D.D., © 2018 by Schmul Publishing Co., Nicholasville, Kentucky. Used by permission."

Cover image copyright: <a href='https://www.123rf.com/profile_niserin'>niserin / 123RF Stock Photo</a>. Used by permission.

Published by Schmul Publishing Co.
PO Box 776
Nicholasville, KY USA

Printed in the United States of America

ISBN 10: 0-88019-612-2
ISBN 13: 978-0-88019-612-3

Visit us on the Internet at www.wesleyanbooks.com, or order direct from the publisher by calling 800-772-6657, or by writing to the above address.

Contents

Publisher's Preface 7
Preface 10
Introduction 13
Author's Introduction 17

I	Is There a Better Country?	19
II	Immortality — The Soul	31
III	Heaven — A Local, Substantial Place	49
IV	Heaven — Various Theories	62
V	Heaven — A Better Country	83
VI	Heaven — Progress and Employment	94
VII	Heaven — Society, Recognition	110
VIII	Heaven — Home	125
IX	Heaven — Rest	142
X	Heaven — Sources of Happiness	154
XI	Heaven — Negative Descriptions	171
XII	Heaven — Preparations For	180

Publisher's Preface

The hope of Heaven has been part and parcel of the Church from its very beginning. And the same hope illuminated the righteous in the eons before Christ's advent. David asserted that he would eschew the material gains of this world in the confidence that "As for me, I will behold thy face in righteousness: I shall be satisfied when I awake, with thy likeness" (Psalm 17:15). Throughout the ages this has been the expectation of the faithful.

With the coming of the Messiah in the flesh, we are assured of the truth of the pre-Christian believers. Jesus confirmed to his disciples, and all those who would come after them, that "I go to prepare a place for you. And if I go and prepare a place for you, I will come again, and receive you unto myself; that where I am, there ye may be also" (John 14:2,3). Glorious, fabulous, incomprehensible promise! Ever since he returned to sit by the throne of his Father, the driving goal of the Believer has ever been to be where he is. It is the ultimate prize of the Christian.

But that does not mean we have been left with only faint ideas of Heaven's environs, like some glowing celestial haze. Bishop Weaver gathers all the data into one compilation for the encouragement of the Christian.

He does not write to convince the skeptic. This is a volume that is almost esoteric in its mission, to be understood and held fast by those inside the Kingdom of God. While he does draw comparisons and contrasts to outside ancient philosophers and scientists of the day, his goal is ever to build up the Believer with a message to hearten and cheer the pilgrim on the sometimes painful, and always dangerous, route to the capital city of the King of Kings.

In the words of Paul, it is an "eternal weight of glory."

—D. Curtis Hale
Publisher, 2018

DEDICATION

To my colaborers,

BISHOP N. CASTLE, D.D.,
BISHOP E. B. KEPHART, D.D., LL.D.,
BISHOP J. W. HOTT, D.D., LL.D.
and
BISHOP J. S. MILLS, D.D., LL.D.,

with whom I have counseled and toiled
so pleasantly,
this little book is dedicated by the

AUTHOR.

Preface

DEATH DOES NOT end all. The grave does not mark the limit of human existence. The hope which kindles in man's heart as he enters upon life's pilgrimage is not to go out, after a few uneventful days, in everlasting night. Somewhere in the universe, we do not know where, but God knows,

"There is a land of pure delight,
Where saints immortal reign."

So the Word teaches; so reason affirms. The soul, weary of sorrow and trial, cries out for such a country. When the shadows had gathered about the sorrowing son of Uz, and death and the grave stretched themselves athwart his vision as awful realities, he raised the question — a question that has engaged the earnest inquiry of the wisest and best of men of all nations and of all ages — *the greatest of all questions* — "If a man die, shall he live again?" Paul summarizes the answer by telling us that Christ "hath brought life and immortality to light through the gospel."

Is Jesus Christ the Son of God? Did he speak with absolute authority? Did his life and utterances express the will of the Father? Then we have a rock of certainty on which to build our faith and hope.

The doctrine of a *future life* is set forth in the following pages with great clearness and force. The author, so long and favorably known, not only in his own Church, but by others as well, has made a study of this and correlated questions all through his ministry, and now, at the close of his seventy-fifth year, gives this volume to the public as, perhaps, the last that shall ever come from his pen. He does not ask the reader to accept mere theories, based upon human reasoning, respecting questions so vital to the present happiness and eternal well-being of mankind, but appeals directly to the Scriptures as the only authentic source of information relative to the future state. With the Bible closed, all is darkness and uncertainty. Christianity itself is but

"The baseless fabric of a vision."

The Bible open, there beams forth from its every page light and hope and a most blessed assurance. Like Peter he would say, "Lord, to whom shall we go? thou hast the words of eternal life."

The style of the book is easy, yet forceful; the arguments cumulative and discriminating. Those who read it in a devout, thoughtful spirit will be both pleased and edified.

The Bishop has chosen to present his views of heaven or that better country, in twelve different chapters, as follows: (1) Is There a Better Country? (2) Immortality, (3) Heaven—A Local, Substantial Place, (4) Various Theories Concerning the Future, (5) Heaven—A Better Country, (6) Progress and Employment in Heaven, (7) Heaven—Society, Recognition, (8) Heaven—Home, (9) Heaven—A Place of Rest, (10) Heaven—Sources of Happiness, (11) Negative Descriptions, (12) Preparations for Heaven.

Under these heads the discussion is so broadened as to include every question related to and clustering about the great central theme—heaven. This volume is for the common people as well as for ministers, and others of extensive research, and will prove a joy to many a pilgrim as he treads the path of duty to which providence has assigned him. Is the mother grief-stricken because her dear children have been ruthlessly torn by death from her fond embrace? It has a message of joy for her. It tells where those precious jewels are. They are not lost—only "gone before." Is the daily toiler, foot-sore and sweat-stained weary of life's burdens? Is he anxious to lay them down forever? Does he long for rest? This book portrays, in words beautiful and simple, the rest that remains "to the people of God." Are any compassed about with trials which make the very heart sad and sore? Has bodily affliction taken much of the charm and beauty out of this life? Does the way grow dark betimes? To all such the author makes a special appeal. Let them read, "And there shall be no more death, neither sorrow, nor crying, neither shall there be any more pain."

Are there those who, at times, if not all the time, are perplexed with doubts concerning the hereafter? Is it hard for them to believe that heaven is a real, visible, tangible place? Following preconceived notions, are they wont to spiritualize everything that relates to the unseen? If so, this book should receive from them a most careful reading. It represents heaven as a place—as a homelike place; as possessing all the elements and joys of an ideal home—a place where all the good are to meet by and by, see each other face to face, and enjoy each other's fellowship forever. This must be so, since the personality, the will, the intellect, the memory, the emotions—in a word, the real, true man—are carried over and exist beyond this world.

May the blessings of God accompany this message to his people, making it an inspiration and joy to as many as shall read it.

—William M. Weekley
Dayton, Ohio, 1899

INTRODUCTION

"LAND AHEAD!" So shouts the mariner long tossed on an ocean journey. The voice comes from one who has been looking and longing for his home. His journey has led him through dark nights, stormy seas, and dangerous rocks and shoals. He is in no wise sad that he is so soon to leave the ship.

Again, the traveler longs to be where the flowers bloom, the grass grows, bees hum, birds sing. There is nothing but water, water and monotony, on the ocean. The people are all travelers. Nobody wants to stay on the ocean forever. All the passengers look anxiously for the land, and for their homes. It will do to make a journey over the ocean, but who could bear the thought of making his home on the great deep?

Thus it need not awaken wonder that Bishop Weaver should be looking for land ahead. He has been a long time on an ocean journey. His boat must be nearing the shore. It is not strange that he begins to think much of the country promised the faithful pilgrims, nor that he should set himself to find out as definitely as may be, what are the attractions of that home the Father hath promised to all his wandering, weary children. He is not complaining of this life, either the length of it or the treatment he has received. Not at all. *But it must soon end.* Hence this outlook. Others have told him the Journey must end, but none have returned from the other shore, and he feels that whatever good this ocean has done him, the greatest good it can ever do is to land him safely on the shore whither he goes.

Having looked ahead and discovered land, the Bishop halts long enough to tell, in this precious little volume, those of us who are seemingly not quite so near the shore, what he has discovered. He has not only seen land ahead, but the Book of books, when carefully examined, reveals a great deal about that shore—its climate, productions, people, its days without night, its life without death, its health without sickness, its joy and happiness without sorrow. In a word, he has discovered that this world, with all its beauty, wealth, stability, and charms, is but a type of the country which God has prepared for the children he is not ashamed to call his own, for they are redeemed and washed in the blood of his Son.

The Bishop did not take shipping, nor sail at a venture. It was not a haphazard journey. He went forth unlike Abraham, who knew not whither he went; the Bishop intended to journey to the promised land. Like Columbus, his faith inspired him and helped him on and over every obstacle, till to-day, like Moses on Mt. Pisgah, he sees that

> "All o'er those wide-extended plains
>   Shines one eternal day;
> There God, the Sun, forever reigns
>   And scatters night away."

And from this lofty viewpoint he calls once again before he enters within the veil to assure his readers that to his mind the mists touching the immortality of man and the heaven of the saved have cleared away. He would thus encourage all his readers to make the journey—if not now on the way to start at once.

It is possible one man in a million believes that "death ends all."

> "He made many a tack,
> His sails oft shifting, to arrive—
> Dread thought, to arrive at nothing,
> And have being no more."

Possibly some doubt a future life and a heaven prepared for the disciples of Jesus Christ. They think—what a mockery to the soul!—they think they are agnostics, and fail to read the messages of God written in the sky, in the Book, in their souls. Still others look, but see not; they listen, but hear jangling voices; they dream, and wonder whether there is anything better for poor mortals in the world to come. They sometimes imagine there may be an existence beyond the grave, but where, what, by whom appointed, or for what purpose, they have no definite information.

> "To be contents [sic] his natural desire,
> He asks no angel's wing, no seraph's fire."

This is the state of mind of hordes of heathen, and of vast numbers who are civilized, and have, or might have, Bible knowledge on the subject.

The reader will find that the author has no such atheism, infidelity, agnosticism, doubt, or fear touching the great hereafter. He holds in this hand a divine Chart which distinctly marks the boundaries of temporal and spiritual things, of time and eternity, of the mortality and immortality of mankind. He trusts and studies this Chart as a child does his geography, with this difference: Even the child knows his book is man-made, and may have imperfections; the Bishop knows his Chart is divine and infallible.

And so the reader will find in this book the simplicity of the child, the wisdom of the sage, the faith of the saint, and the comfort of one who knows in whom he believes.

"If it were not so, I would have told you," said Jesus; that is, "if there were no life beyond, no resurrection, no home in the skies, no mansions in my Father's house, I have knowledge enough, and goodness enough, and love enough, to have told you that death is an eternal sleep. But there *is* such a life, such a home. I myself go to prepare it, and will come again to receive you and bid you welcome to all the glory of my Father's house."

Reader, peruse this book, and see if it does not draw you nearer to the great white throne.

—W<small>M</small>. M<small>C</small>K<small>EE</small>
Dayton, Ohio

Author's Introduction

Heaven, immortality, and eternal life mutually imply each other, and mean more to mankind than all other subjects combined. What question can be so far-reaching and of such solemn importance to a rational, intelligent being as that which directly relates to his future, endless, unalterable condition? There is nothing in time, nor in all the range of human thought, that is worthy to be compared with it. The author of this little book, while he is not indifferent to the views and opinions of critics, schoolmen, and metaphysicians, has not conferred with them, but has sought in a plain, simple manner to present the subject in its different phases, as suggested by reason and revelation. Each chapter, while it is not out of harmony with any other chapter, is, nevertheless, in a measure independent. This seemed to be the better way to treat the subject as a whole. Oftentimes the same text of Scripture or the same argument or illustration that bears upon one phase of the subject, bears with equal force and directness upon some other phase of the same subject.

Heaven is presented to our view in the sacred Scriptures,

not only by precept, but in images, figures, and symbols. Looking at heaven through the Bible is like looking into a well-arranged prism; every turn you give it, however slight, gives some new and beautiful combination of colors. It may appear to the reader that there is here and there an unnecessary amount of repetition, when, in fact, it is only a slight turn of the heavenly prism, giving a different glimpse of the same subject.

The author, in his own not very attractive style, has sought to bring before the mind of the reader as clear ideas of the future state of the saints as it was possible for him to do. He is fully aware of the lack of literary finish, but hopes that it may be helpful and encouraging to at least a few of the pilgrim sojourners who are seeking for, and earnestly desiring to find, that better country. May it be that on some glad day, when the clouds are lifted and the mists have rolled away, the reader and the writer will find a home in the Father's house of many mansions. With the hope that some wayfaring pilgrim may be helped on his way toward the city of the living God, this unpretending little book is given to the public by the

—AUTHOR

I
Is There a Better Country?

> "The soul, secured in her existence, smiles
> At the drawn dagger, and defies its point.
> The stars shall fade away, the sun himself
> Grow dim with age, and Nature sink in years;
> But thou shalt flourish in immortal youth,
> Unhurt amidst the war of elements,
> The wrecks of matter, and the crash of worlds."

WE ARE EVER in the midst of inexplicable mysteries. In the sea, in the land, in the heavens above us, and the atmosphere around us—in whatever direction we turn our thoughts we shall meet with something we do not understand. We know, or may know something about many things, but the wisest philosophers did not, and could not know all about anything. Paul never uttered a truer sentiment than when he said, "For now we see through a glass darkly... now I know in part." But it is only in part. We have glimpses, but no more. Just beyond where our investigations have carried us, are vast fields that we have not so much as entered. The astronomer has gone far out into the heavens, and brought back much interesting and valuable information concerning the size, distance, and motion of the heavenly bodies. He tells us about the centrifugal and centripetal forces by which worlds and systems of worlds are held within certain grooves, while they rush along many thousands of miles an hour. But with all the information he brings us he comes asking many questions: Are there not other worlds and systems beyond those we have discovered? Have we reached the very corner of the universe? Is not the Milky Way but the glimmering of stars and planets too distant to be reached by the telescope? When and for what purpose were all those worlds made? Are any of them inhabited? If so, with what order of beings? Are they superior or inferior to man? What do they know about God? What is their form of worship? Have they fallen as man fell? Have they been redeemed? What do they know about us? What communication have they with the inhabitants of other worlds? These and a thousand other like questions must remain unanswered until we shall have passed out of this shadowy region.

But, coming to things with which we seem to be more familiar, we shall find that we are hemmed in on every side. We can see in part, but it is only in part. We are conscious that we live, but who can tell us what life is? We see evidences of it all about us, but what is it? Dr. Harbaugh says: "It is not motion; it is not influence. These are effects of life, but not life itself. It is nothing material. It is not heat. In the tree it is not root, sap, bark, wood, limb, leaf, flower, fruit, nor all these combined. It is not the power which combines and animates them. In the animal frame it is not skin, muscle, flesh, bone, nor all these together. In intellectual beings it is not understanding, will, affections, passions, nor the union of all these. What then is life? It is deeper than all effects. It is an *invisible general law,* lying beneath and behind all manifestations; the hidden, quiet, powerful, and mysterious basis of all tangible being." It is "so delicate, so feeble, so dependent upon the fostering circumstances and the kindly care of nature, yet so invisible; endowed as with supernatural powers, like spirits of the air, which yield to every touch, and seem to elude our force... Life, weakest and strangest of the things God has made, is the heir of Death, and yet his conqueror—victim and victor. All living things succumb to Death's assault. Life smiles at his impotence and makes the grave her cradle."

Joseph Cook defines life in physical organisms to be, "the power which coordinates the movements of general matter." D. D. Whedon, LL.D., defines it to be: "That state of organic matter which is necessary to its becoming the basis of intelligence. Or, more briefly, life is the organic condition of thought." Then we have Darwin, with his "Natural Selection," Huxley with his "Protoplasm," and Spencer with his "Universal Evolution." To these may be added the various opinions of many of the philosophers, from Aristotle to Bastian. Concerning "Spontaneous Generation," Rev. J. H. Potts, A.M., says, "Futile has been every effort to penetrate into the mysterious temple of life in order to lay bare its principle, and the greatest philosopher approaches no nearer than the crowd." Professor L. L. Beal, of King's College, London, a learned physiologist, says: "Notwithstanding all that has been asserted to the contrary, not one vital action has yet been accounted for by physics and chemistry. The assertion that life is correlated forces rests upon assertion alone, and we are just as far from an explanation of vital phenomena by the force hypothesis as we were before the discovery of the doctrine of correlation of forces."

After all that has been said by philosophers, scientists,

and physiologists, life in itself is an inexplicable mystery. "We take our stand," says Rev. J. H. Potts, "on the broad, safe, and scriptural platform that Omnipotence alone is adequate to produce life. Spontaneous generation, like perpetual motion, is a thing unknown. The scientist who searches for the one is equally vain with the philosopher who labors for the other. Let it be affirmed, with the great and good Agassiz, that 'it is necessary that we recur to a cause more exalted, and recognize influences more powerful, exercising over all nature an action more direct, if we would not move eternally in a vicious circle.'"

But it is not life only that is a mystery; the inexplicables are all around us. Who can tell us all about the law of gravitation, the properties of light and heat, the true philosophy of sound and motion, and a thousand other forces and properties in nature? Lavater, in speaking of mysteries, says, "Each particle of matter is an immensity, each leaf a world, each insect an inexplicable compendium." T. Adams says, "Sinful man, saved in Christ, is, always was, and always will be a mystery, a wonder." Evans says: "Happy is the man who is content to traverse this ocean to the haven of rest without going into the wretched diving-bells of his own fancies. There are depths, but depths are for God." Bishop Hall says: "I would fain know all I need, and all that I may. I leave God's secrets to himself. It is happy for me that God makes me of his court, and not of his council."

Man is a mystery in himself, and to himself. David said, "I am fearfully and wonderfully made." Whether he alludes to man physically, mentally, or morally, or all combined, it is true that he is "fearfully and wonderfully made." Dr. Hillis says, "Men go toward death starred with latent faculties and forces, just as our winterbound earth goes toward May starred with myriad germs and seeds, waiting for summer to unlock and send them forth to bud, and blossom, and fruitage." There are unexplored riches in the human constitution. What is man? No one knows. Many of his faculties exist in him like wrapped tools in a box, not even examined, much less named. "Three or four of his forty faculties ask threescore years for development; the other latent powers ask an immortal life for growth and development." If death ends all, what need of these faculties? Life is too short to develop them, and if there is no life beyond, they will perish before they are used. Would a wise and benevolent Creator bestow faculties upon man, and then withhold from him the necessary time and opportunity to develop them? Reason lifts her voice against the theory of annihilation.

Death is also a mystery. We know something of its effects from the earth side, but what do we know of the other side? We know that "man dieth and wasteth away," "dust to dust, and ashes to ashes." But that is not death. We know that in death there is a separation between soul and body, and that physical life ceases. But what is death? We know many things by experience, but not having passed that way, we do not and cannot know what death is, nor what it is to die. We have said that life is a mystery; and even so death is a mystery.

"If," says Rev. John Reid, "a saved or lost man were to come among us from eternity, we would question him thus: What was it to die? Did it seem like going into a sleep, or were you distinctly conscious? When the soul had left the body, how did you feel? If you went to a place of punishment, what was your experience on the journey? Did evil spirits conduct you to the door of the prison of woe? Can you give us any definite conception of the miseries of the lost? Or, if you went to heaven, what were your feelings on the way? How many of the celestial inhabitants accompanied you? How did they appear, and what did they say? In what way do spirits convey their thoughts to each other? How did you feel when you entered the city of God? Who met you first—Christ, angels, or your departed friends? Is it possible for you to describe the appearance of the God-man? What is the nature of the glorified bodies of Enoch and Elijah? As it respects the blessedness and employment of the saved, can you make us understand the simple truth in the case? What peculiar divine glory fills heaven, and what is meant by the vision of God? Many other questions we might ask, but there is no one to answer them. At the end of all our inquiries we have to sigh. Great leading thoughts relating to the future state are all that God has favored us with. A degree of dimness is meant to cloud that wonderful region of life."

Thus, in life and death, as well as in the whole realm of nature, there are so many mysteries; is it any great marvel that there should be at least some mysteries concerning a state or condition upon which we have not entered? The wisest and best among the old philosophers, notwithstanding their deep penetration, were willing to allow this. When man shall have solved all the mysteries in the realm of nature, it will then be time for him to demand that the gate leading into the beyond be thrown open, and he be permitted to read and understand the "vision of God." But, if the "vision of God" were flashed upon man in his present state, even if he could survive such a revelation, it would wholly unfit him for the duties of this life. "All the studies and pursuits, the arts and labors, which now employ the activity of man, which support the order, or promote the happiness of society, would lie neglected and abandoned." The infinite God has a purpose in all he does. That man should be kept on a state of probation for a time, with only occasional glimpses of what there is beyond, is God's plan.

To know that there is a better country, with environments infinitely superior to those with which we are now surrounded, and that we may enter into it, ought to make us contented with our lot. But the proud skeptic turns away from the Holy Scriptures, rejects the voice of his own conscience, and then looks into the cold, stony face of nature and exclaims, "I see no evidence in nature of anything beyond this life." If he knew himself better, and knew how to read nature rightly, he would have fewer doubts concerning a future state. Nature is full of analogies pointing toward death, the resurrection of the dead, and a future state; but these can only be traced clearly when the light of revelation shines upon them. Columbus, from his knowledge of geography, believed that there was another continent. The astronomer, from what he has seen of the motion of the heavenly bodies, believes there are other planets. Columbus was not disappointed; nor has the astronomer been mislead [sic], for ever and anon a new star or planet has been discovered. So man, if he will awake to the facts within and all about him, must believe that something remains for him after this life. But the pride of human reason is offended when asked to accept as true anything mysterious in spiritual existence, but turns around and bows complacently to the inexplicable in material things.

Wonderful and mysterious as life is, all intelligent beings love it. It were a sin not to love life; and as long as right reason occupies the throne this love of life will continue. No sane man will wantonly destroy his own life. "All that a man hath will he give for his life." A dying queen said, "Millions of money for an inch of time." To thoughtful persons no theory is more unwelcome than that of annihilation. Our whole being revolts at the cold, cheerless thought of ceasing to exist. "For where is the difference," asks Seneca, the Stoic, "between not beginning to be at all, and ceasing to exist? The effect of both is the same—not to be." If there is any difference, it were better not to be at all, than to be, and then cease to be. If there be nothing after this life, then nothing awaits us but annihilation—eternal silence. Approaching the end of this life with nothing to hope for beyond, is not only gloomy and cheerless, but indescribably horrid. An infidel in his last moments was urged by his friends who were standing by to hold on to his theory, and not surrender, as they feared he might do. He turned to them and said, "Gentlemen, I have no objection to holding on if you will tell me what to hold to." Life was gone, nothing beyond; hence, nothing to hold to. "I am taking a leap into the dark," were the last words of the infidel Hobbs. "I am abandoned of God and man," were the pitiful words of Voltaire. Similar words were uttered by Lord Byron, Altamont, and other noted infidels. What does all this mean? If death ends all, why such feelings in the last moments of life? William Hunter, when dying, said, "All is well, all is well." Parsons said, "Victory, victory, in the blood of the Lamb!" Robert Newton said: "I am going, going to glory! Farewell sin; farewell death! Praise the Lord!"

Thousands of such dying testimonies are upon the record. Why this difference between infidels and Christians? What does it all mean? Is there no lesson in it? If the notion of a better country is all a delusion, then it is a most delightful delusion in which to close the last hour of mental existence. Some such delusion must have captured the mind of Balaam when he said, "Let me die the death of the righteous, and let my last end be like his!" Why?

The thirst of man in all the ages has been, and now is, for something better. No matter what his environments are, he is not satisfied. Solomon in all his glory was not satisfied. Again and again he exclaimed, "Vanity of vanities, all is vanity!" The children of Israel, to whom the Lord had promised the land of Canaan, were longing, hoping, and sighing for that goodly land. In the fullness of time, they were triumphantly led across the Jordan and put in possession of that promised land. They found it to be, in every respect, just such a country as the Lord had promised. They drank of its waters and milk, ate of its honey and fruits, but were they satisfied? No. For Paul says, "Now they desired a better country." Thus it is, and always has been with man. Whence this unrest, this dissatisfaction?

If there is nothing beyond this world for man, then there

is a great defect somewhere. Where is it? what is it? and who is responsible for it? Let reason take the throne and give a solution. "Nature," says Dr. Binney, "never deceives." All the instincts, all the faculties which are in any of its creatures—there is always something to meet them. Nature does not disappoint. If there is a particular appetite, there is something to meet it; if there is a particular faculty, there is something to meet it; if there is a particular instinct, there is something to meet it. Well, then, the moral aspirations of man, the spiritual instincts, the irrepressible anticipations of which he is capable, and which are in him, part of himself,—faculties and instincts which nature has bestowed,—is she to play fast and loose with them? Is she to deceive him with regard to them? She deceives in nothing beside. She meets every appetite and instinct of inferior creatures,—she meets them with that which is appropriate; but the highest affections, the noblest aspirations, the spiritual instincts, are they all make-believes? Is nature deceiving and tantalizing man in all that?

No matter what our notions of man may be, whether we believe that he is altogether mortal or partly immortal, the fact remains that there are in him aspirations and longings for something better and higher than he has yet found in this world. He may hide away in some deep, dark cavern of the earth, where the light of the midday sun cannot reach him, but he cannot get away from his own consciousness. The materialist may say that this is begging the question, but it is not; it is the setting of facts over against theory. The facts are that man has, and always did have these aspirations, instincts, and longings for something better—a conscious conviction that there must be something for man after this life. The theory is that all these are false, that his individual consciousness is a delusion, to go down, with all his instincts, aspirations, and longings into everlasting silence. On what basis does this heartless, soulless theory rest? Who can explain it? It leaves man in mid-ocean without chart or compass, and only laughs to see him sink in fathomless water.

> "Who reads his lesson reads immortal life;
> Or nature there, imposing on her sons,
> Has written fables—man was made to lie."

If God created man, it is easy to understand that when he breathed into him the breath of life, and he became a living soul, he also breathed into him the aspirations for, and the consciousness of, some better things to come; but if man came from nobody knows where, and nobody knows how, who can explain the mystery of his instincts, aspirations, and longings? If this expectation of an existence after this life was a local tradition, limited to one age, and to one people, we might attribute it to some bias of the mind or temporary cause; but what shall we say when confronted with the fact that it is limited to no age, and is as universal as the family of man? A belief so general must have a substantial basis, and it is not unphilosophical to say that it must be true.

If we accept the Holy Scriptures as a revelation from God, the doctrine of a future state is at once and forever settled. "The arguments founded upon reason and nature are not in themselves absolutely conclusive." At the same time, there is nothing in the doctrine of a future life that contradicts either reason or nature. Socrates, after arguing in favor of a future state, says, "It would seem most reasonable to believe that some such thing were true." While it is not our purpose in this chapter to discuss the doctrine of a future state by arguments drawn from the Scriptures, yet we think it proper to state a few things. One of the richest blessings God ever bestowed upon the world is a revelation concerning himself and the future destiny of man. Philosophers and poets of the long ago often talked of a future state, but not being able to prove it beyond all doubt, their brightest utterances were often overshadowed by that cheerless word "if." In the midst of this dread uncertainty God, in his infinite kindness, gave to man a revelation without an "if." "It is," says Rev. J. H. Potts, "especially assuring and comforting to know that the deductions of ancient philosophers, guided only by the light of reason, and the dreams of ancient poets, gathering up the traditions of the long ago, are all in substantial agreement with what the prophets and evangelists wrote and spoke when moved by the Holy Spirit." Reason, revelation, and nature, when rightly interpreted, are in the most perfect harmony with each other. Poor man, blinded and bewildered by the awful effects of sin, with only glimpses of what there is in nature, cannot with absolute certainty know what there is beyond this life. To settle this tremendous question and give a reasonable solution of the aspirations, yearnings, and instincts of the human soul, the infinite and merciful Creator gave to man a revelation concerning another life, with all necessary instructions how to secure it. This blessed Book! — "a rock of diamonds and chain of pearls; a chart by which we may sail into the harbor of peace" — "without it we should be like benighted travelers seeking our way in a dreary wood, bewildered rather than aided by the mimic lights that play around us in the dismal bogs." Sir Isaac Newton said, "We account the Scriptures of God to be the most sublime philosophy." It teaches the way to live and the way to die.

The astronomer, aided by his telescope, reaches out into the heavens far beyond the range of our natural vision, and discovers worlds and systems of worlds, and allows that there may be many others in the far-away realm of space; but he cannot tell whether any of the worlds seen or unseen are inhabited. But the Scriptures go beyond all these outworks of creation, enter the central empire of the universe, and give a glowing description of its magnitude, beauty, and glory. No questions as to whether or not it is inhabited! There are cherubim, and seraphim, and an innumerable company of angels, and the spirits of just men made perfect—all perfect, all happy, all contented and satisfied. Is not that infinitely and altogether better and far more in harmony with the aspirations, instincts, and longings of the human soul, than the cold, dreary, and repulsive theory of annihilation?

> "Oh, listen, man!
> A voice within us speaks that startling word,
> 'Man, thou shalt never die.' Celestial voices
> Hymn it into our souls; according harps,
> By angel fingers touched, when the mild stars
> Of morning sang together, sound forth still
> The song of our great immortality."

II
IMMORTALITY — THE SOUL

"To be, or not to be: that is the question...
To sleep: perchance to dream: ay, there's the rub."

"Whence springs this pleasing hope, this fond desire
This longing after immortality?
Or whence this secret dread and inward horror
Of falling into naught? Why shrinks the soul
Back on herself, and startles at destruction?"

THE DOCTRINE OF the immortality of man is one of the most pleasing and elevating doctrines that ever engaged the human thought. What if there are inexplicable mysteries involved in it; that cannot be accepted as a valid argument against it. We know that life is a fact, notwithstanding the mystery about it. No one can tell what life is. Death is a fact, but not without a mystery. So in every nook and corner in the whole realm of nature there are mysteries. Which is the greater mystery, to live forever or to live at all? Which is the more desirable, to live forever or to cease to live? There is a majesty, a grandeur, in the thought of immortality that sends a thrill to the very heart of man. Who can think seriously of an endless conscious existence and not feel impressed with a sense of his own greatness? Empires, kingdoms, and republics rise, and fall, and pass away; but man—immortal man—lives on. Living and moving among the dying and the dead, and yet ever conscious that there is something within that will survive the dissolution of the body, is not a humiliating thought; and when considered in the light of reason and sound philosophy it is uplifting and desirable. To enter upon a state of endless progression, under the most favorable conditions, and without the thought of extinction or change other than that of increased and ever-increasing pleasure and delight, brings to the human consciousness a degree of satisfaction and comfort not found in the cold and cheerless theory of annihilation. How could the gods be so cruel as to breathe into the consciousness of man the hope and aspiration for an endless existence and then dash them to pieces on the very threshold of their realization. The Father of Lights will not treat his children thus.

While plodding through this world of sin and sorrow, where everything is imperfect, and death and dissolution is written upon every living thing, we can do no better than see through a glass darkly. We can see in part, but it is only in part—faint glimpses, and no more; sin has dimmed everything. The brain is too heavy and sluggish to think rapidly, the eyes are too dim to see clearly, and the ear is too dull to hear properly. The mind works under great disadvantages, so that progress, of necessity, must be slow. But in that better country the brain will be as ether, the vision clear, the hearing acute, and the environments perfect.

If man as we find him is not altogether immoral, neither

is he altogether mortal. He has instincts, thoughts, hopes, and aspirations which do not and cannot inhere in matter alone. There is no form in which matter exists where we find the same elements and forces that we find in man. He not only stands alone, but above everything else on earth. What gives him this superiority? Dr. Bushnell says: "I cannot believe that earth is man's abiding-place. It can't be that our life is cast up by the ocean of eternity to float a moment upon its waves and then sink into nothingness; else why is it that the glorious aspirations which leap like angels from the temple of our hearts are ever wandering about unsatisfied? Why is it that the rainbow and clouds come over us with a beauty that is not of earth and then pass off and leave us to muse upon their favored loveliness? Why is it that the stars, which hold their festivals around the midnight throne, are set above the grasp of our limited faculties, forever mocking us with their unapproachable glory? And, finally, why is it that bright forms of human beauty are presented to our view and then taken from us, leaving the thousand streams of our affections to flow in Alpine torrents upon our hearts? We are born for a higher destiny than that of earth. There is a realm where the rainbow never fades, where the stars will be spread before us like islands that slumber on the ocean, and where the beings that pass before us like a shadow will stay in our presence forever."

However lightly and indifferently skeptics and scientists may treat the doctrine of consciousness, the fact remains that some suh thing inheres in man. It is part of himself, and he cannot get rid of it, however hard he may try. Whether you say that it is a creature of education or an innate something is immaterial, so far as this subject is concerned; but if it is wholly a creature of education, the marvel is that all men in all the ages should have been taught so nearly alike concerning a future state. No matter what their surroundings may be, or may have been; no matter how vague and unreasonable their opinions may be, they all believe in some sort of existence after this life. Have we any evidence that the horse, or any other purely animal being, has any such instinct? There is in every human soul, whether mortal or immortal, the abiding conviction that, somewhere in the universe, there is a Being superior to man, and that man, in some form or other, will exist after this life. This is, and has been, the dream of all the nations and peoples of the earth as far back as we can trace the history of man. Whence this conviction, this universal belief? Some have attributed it to the teaching of the Scriptures. Now, while we are glad to admit that the doctrine is clearly taught in the Bible, yet this does not account for the origin and universality of this belief for two reasons: First, the writers of the sacred Scriptures must have believed it, else they would not have written it. Whence came their belief? Second, it is believed by nations and peoples that never saw nor heard of the Bible. Whence their belief? If only those who have, and have had access to the Scriptures believed in the future existence of man, this might be admitted as the history of its origin; but such is not the fact, and hence it must be accounted for in some other way.

Bishop J. S. Mills says: "My faith in man's immortality rests upon three facts:

"1. The natural *instinct of immortality* in every soul.

> "A solemn murmur in the soul
> Tells of the world to be,
> As travelers hear the billows roll
> Before they reach the sea.

"2. The voice of Christian consciences, as expressed by Paul: 'After that ye believed, ye were sealed with the Holy Spirit of promise, which is the earnest of our inheritance.'

"3. Jesus Christ—his character, life, words, and deeds.

Whoever holds these no more needs other evidence than did Elijah when ascending to heaven in a chariot of fire."

If the belief of the immortality and future existence of man obtained only among the most degraded and stupid nations, tribes, and peoples of the earth, we might say that it was only a low and vulgar superstition; or, if it were believed only by the most learned and enlightened men and nations, then we might say that it was nothing more than a clever fancy or speculation. But what shall we say when the wisest and best men and nations of all the ages, past and present, believe it? It remains for the few who reject the doctrine to give a reasonable account of the origin and universality of the belief.

Lord Bolingbroke, a learned infidel, says: "The doctrine of the immortality of the soul and a future state of rewards and punishments began to be taught before we have any light into antiquity. And when we begin to have any, we find it established that it was strongly inculcated from time immemorial, and as early as the most ancient and learned nations appear to us."

Dr. Leland says: "We find that it equally obtained among the most barbarous as among the most civilized nations. The ancient Scythians, Indians, Gauls, Germans, Britons, as well as the Greeks and Romans, believed that souls are immortal and that man shall live in another state after death."

Dr. Dick, in his philosophy of a future state, says: "That the thinking principle in man is an immortal nature was believed by the ancient Egyptians, the Persians, the Phoenicians, the Scythians, the Celts, the Druids, the Assyrians, by the wisest and most celebrated characters among the Greeks and Romans, and by almost every other nation and tribe whose records have reached our times."

Dr. Harbaugh says: "The ancient nations and tribes have always somewhere located for themselves a heaven as the object of their hopes. The spiritual longings of the superstitious pagans found a home for their dead beyond the misty sea. There, in some island, unknown and unvisited by mortals, their imagination located the Hesperian gardens and Elysian fields."

Of the Indians he says: "They believe that beyond the most distant mountains of their country there is a wide river; beyond that river a great country; on the other side of that country a world of water; in that water are a thousand islands full of trees and streams of water, and that a thousand buffaloes and ten thousand deer graze on the hills or ruminate in the valleys. When they die they are persuaded that the Great Spirit will conduct them to their land of souls."

"Even the poor Indian, whose untutored mind sees God in clouds, or hears him in the wind, —

> "Whose soul proud science never taught to stray
> Far as the solar walk or milky way—
> Yet simple nature to his hopes has given,
> Behind the cloud-capt hill, an humble heaven:
> Some safer world in depths of wood embase,
> Some happier island in the watery waste,
> Where slaves once more their native land behold,
> No fiends torment in Christian's thirst for gold—
> And thinks, admitted to yon equal sky,
> This faithful dog shall bear him company."

However crude and unreasonable these pagan notions may appear to us, they all stand as presumptive evidence of the immortality of man. Our purpose in using them so freely in this connection is to show that man, find him as you may, has within him the abiding conviction that there is something for him beyond death. To what has been given may be added the notions and opinions of the Magian sect which prevailed in Babylonia, Media, Assyria, and Persia; as also the doctrine taught by Zoroaster, who lived in the time of Darius, and as the nations, tribes, and people of the long ago believed in the immortality and future existence of man, so there is scarcely a nation, or tribe, or people at this day but that holds the same opinion. Man can but ill afford to live and die in doubt in matters pertaining to this life alone, and he can neither afford to live nor die in doubt concerning his future destiny. Of all questions within the range of human thought none can be of greater importance than that which relates to the future endless condition of the soul. Where, and under what conditions shall I spend my eternity?

It is very generally admitted that the philosophers and poets of Greece and Rome believed in the future endless existence of man. Socrates, a little while before his death, said, "When the dead are arisen at the rendezvous of departed souls, whither their angel conducts them, they are all judged." Again he said, "I am in good hopes that there is something for those that are dead, and that, as hath been said of old, 'it is much better for good than for bad men.'" Plato said, "We ought always to believe the ancient and sacred words [which plainly point to some traditions of great antiquity, and are supposed to be of divine origin] which show both that the soul is immortal and that it hath judges, and suffers the greatest punishment when it is disengaged from the body." Aristotle, as cited by Plutarch, speaking of the happiness of men after their departure out of this life, represents it as a most ancient opinion, so old that no man knew when it began or who was the author of it, that it hath been handed down to us by tradition from infinite ages. Cicero argues in favor of the immortality of the soul from the consent of all nations to it. He says it was believed "by those of the best authority, which in every case is and ought to be of great weight; and that all the ancients agreed in it who were the more worthy of credit and the more likely to know the truth the nearer they approached to the first rise of mankind and to their divine origin."

Seneca, Plutarch, and many others of the philosophers might be cited as holding substantially the same opinions as these already given. The poems of Homer, Ovid, and Virgil "contain a variety of descriptions, in which the same opinions are involved." How shall we account for this general belief in the immortality and future existence of man? Suppose the belief that "death ends all" were as universal as the belief that it does not end all, what would a philosopher say? If we say it is only a tradition, handed down through the ages from the remotest antiquity, we still ask when and with whom it originated. It must have had an origin. If we say it is intuition, then we ask again, By whom, or in what manner, was this strange intuition implanted in the consciousness of all mankind? Is nature so cruelly false to herself as to play such a game with man? Dr. Leland, who made this subject a study for years, says, "The most reasonable account which can be given of the early and universal spreading of the doctrine of a future state among the nations, is that it was a part of the primitive religion communicated to the first parents and ancestors of the human race, and which came originally by divine revelation, and was by them transmitted to their posterity." Grotius, when speaking concerning the immortality and future existence of man, says, "This most ancient tradition spread from our first parents (for from whom else could it come?) to almost all civilized nations." But account for the origin and universality of the belief of mankind in a future state as you may, there is something in it which more nearly conforms to the longings, instincts, and aspirations in man than in all other theories combined. It is said that Clembratus, a heathen, after reading the discourses of Plato upon the immortality of the soul, cast himself headlong from a high rock and broke his neck, that he might the sooner enter upon that immortality which he loved, and believed would follow after death.

Cicero says: "If I am wrong in believing the souls of men

immortal, I please myself in my mistake; nor while I live will I ever choose that this opinion with which I am so much delighted, should ever be wrested from me. But if at death I am to be annihilated, as some philosophers suppose, I am not afraid lest those wise men, when extinct too, should laugh at my error."

Plato says : "'When, therefore, death comes upon man, what is mortal in him perishes, as it is seen to do; but what is immortal withdraws itself from death safe and uncorrupted."

"Never," says Dr. Blair, "has any nation been discovered on the face of the earth, so rude and barbarous that in the midst of their wildest superstitions there was not cherished among them some expectation of a state after death in which the virtuous were to enjoy happiness."

Bishop E. B. Kephart, D.D., says: "Man finds himself in a state where change is ever and everywhere; all things are in a flux, life here, death there, production and reproduction and decay run their ceaseless round. But in all this bewilderment no trace of annihilation is manifest; life springs out of death, and beauty out of decay. Man's chief concern is with the future, and he cannot think of a moment in the unmeasured eternity before him in which he is not interested. This desire is not limited to his earth-life, but is boundless; his plans and his purposes are not completed here; surely this uniform disposition of the mind is not a mere vagary. Can it be that the deepest intuition of the human soul deceives us? No, the conscious being in which this prophetic intuition inheres must continue to be, to feel, to think, to act forever. I cannot think that God who implanted this intuition will deceive me; he cannot but be true.

"But, speaking scientifically, there is not one organism within the realms of matter that is not the direct product of life. It is always life first and organism afterwards. Then why should we conclude, when the organism becomes broken and life departs, that the living agent has become extinct. To do so is unscientific. But in God's Word we have the only sure word of prophecy."

Modern skeptics, driven by their own consciousness, right reason, sound philosophy, and the overwhelming testimony of all nations, tribes, and peoples of the earth, past and present, have taken shelter in the dilapidated hovel of Gnosticism, where their creed, when carried to the last analysis, may be summed up in three words, "I DON'T KNOW."

The dying testimony of Christians, while it is not an infallible proof of the immortality of the soul and the future existence of man, furnishes a strong presumptive evidence that "it is not all of life to live" here. If man is ever honest in expressing his hopes and fears, it is most likely to be in the hour of his dissolution. Rev. J. H. Potts, A.M., says: "If the soul of man were only a breath, if life were only a spark, which expires when the heart ceases to beat, would there not have been an experience of the waning flame? Would there not have been at least one testimony in the six thousand years, among the thousands of millions of dying men, going to show a *conscious nearness* to oblivion? But there is not one such, not one."

Suppose that thousands of millions of the wisest and best men on earth, when dying, would have said, "I am sinking into utter nothingness," what would a philosopher say? Would he not say that it furnishes a strong presumptive proof that "death ends all"? What should he say when the testimony is all on the other side?

Because the soul is immortal and cannot cease to exist, we must not hence infer that all souls will be happy after death. Immortality and eternal blessedness do not immutably imply each other. We cannot cease to be, but as free moral agents we can fix the conditions under which that endless existence will be continued. As we sow, so shall we reap.

Long ago some one said, "Let me die the death of the

righteous, and let my last end be like his!" Why? Because "the righteous hath hope in his death." A young lady, whose father was an infidel and whose mother was a Christian, as she drew near to death, turned to her father, who was standing by her bed, and asked, "Father, in whose faith shall I die?" With deep emotion he said, "Daughter, die in your mother's faith." Mary Queen of Scots, just before her execution, said, "Like as thy arms were stretched out upon the cross, even so receive me within the stretched-out arms of thy mercy." Kneeling down and bareing [sic] her neck to the executioner, she exclaimed, "My God, I have hoped in thee—into thy hands I commit myself!" Among the last words of Jane, Queen of Navarre, were these, "God, by this sickness, calls me hence to enjoy a better life; and now I shall enter into the desired haven toward which this frail vessel of mine has been a long time steering." During the last days of John Wesley he repeated several times, "The best of all is, God is with us." Toplady's last words were, "It will not be long before God takes me, for no mortal man can live after the glories which God has manifested to my soul." Rutherford said: "Christ is mine, and I am his. Glory to my Creator and Redeemer forever! Glory shines in Immanuel's land. Oh, for arms to embrace him! Oh, for a well-tuned harp!" Whitefield said, "Peace! peace! victory!" Dr. Eddy said: "Dying is a fact—that takes care of itself. Faith in the great hereafter, through Christ, is my strength." His last words were: "Hallelujah! hallelujah! sing and pray—eternity dawns." Philip William Otterbein said, "I begin to feel an unspeakable fullness of love and peace divine." An aged lady, when dying, said to her son, a minister, who was standing by her bed and had just asked how it appeared to her, "I think I must be half-way over, and it is all glory." Ten thousand times ten thousand such testimonies have been given. What does it all mean? Does it mean that there is no God—nothing beyond this life—and that nature is simply playing a stupendous trick on man?

Or, does it mean that the Creator is forming these aspirations, instincts, and hopes, only to crush them at last? Oh, it cannot be!

Rev. W. R. Funk, D.D., says: "To live always, is the soul's fondest desire, its highest hope. To be with God and his Son, our Saviour, is worth every effort. Immortality! If we could count the leaves of every forest and mark every blade of grass in the universe, and if this earth were a heap of sand and every grain numbered, we might multiply these together and the soul's immortal life would have only begun, even if each leaf, blade, and grain stood for one thousand years. The thought of spending this neverending state of bliss with Jesus is an inspiration, and its realization will be peace, joy, happiness, glory, and eternal life."

Omitting some of the metaphysical arguments used by philosophers and theologians in proof of the immortality and future endless existence of the soul, we turn directly to the Holy Scriptures, where the doctrine is clearly and abundantly taught.

> "Within this awful volume lies
> The mystery of mysteries.
> Oh, happiest they of human race
> To whom our God has given grace
> To hear, to read, to fear, to pray,
> To lift the latch and force the way;
> But better had they ne'er been born
> Who read to doubt, or read to scorn."

It is exceedingly comforting and assuring to know that reason, consciousness, and revelation are all in the most perfect harmony with each other. Only a few of the many passages bearing upon the future destiny of man can be given in this connection. From Moses sat the burning bush to John on the isle of Patmos the doctrine is taught. The Lord said to Moses, "I am the God of thy father, the God of Abraham, the God of Isaac, and the God of Jacob." Our Lord, in quoting and explaining this passage, says, "He is not the God of the dead, but the God of the living," thus teaching us that although Abraham, Isaac, and Jacob had ceased to live on the earth for hundreds of years, they were still living. If Jesus had said that God *was* not the God of the dead, but of the living, it would change the sense of the passages; but he puts it in the present tense by saying that God *is* not the God of the dead, but of the living. Upon this text Dr. Clark says, "Our Lord combats and refutes the opinion of the Sadducees, who say *there is neither angel nor spirit,* by showing that the *soul* is not only immortal, but lives with God, even *while* the *body* is detained in the *dust* of the *earth.*" Job says, "I *know* that my redeemer liveth, and that he shall stand at the latter day upon the earth: and though after my skin worms destroy this body, yet in my flesh shall I see God." Two cardinal doctrines are taught in this passage: first, the resurrection of the dead; and second, the future existence of man. *"I shall see God."* I shall see him for myself. There is a deep meaning in that personal pronoun "I," which he afterward explains to mean himself. "I shall see for myself." Closely allied to this are the words of the psalmist, "The days of our years are threescore years and ten; and if by reason of strength they be fourscore years, yet is their strength labour and sorrow; for it is soon cut off, and *we* flyaway." What flies away? Not the body, for that remains. Not the years nor the strength, for they are cut off. It is the *we* that flies away, the real self. Shortly before Socrates died some of his friends asked what they should do with him after he was dead. He told them that if they could *catch* him they should do thus and so. He did not believe that Socrates would be there. As in the case of Lazarus, while the town people buried what they could see, they did not bury Lazarus; for he was off with the angels. What a thrilling thought this is! We do not and cannot see the man. The *we*—the *self*, the *man*—is inside of what we see. And it is this undying *we* that flies away.

Again, the psalmist says: "Thou shalt guide me with thy counsel, and afterward receive me to glory... My flesh and my heart faileth: but God is the strength of my heart, and my portion for ever." It was not the present that gave him strength and comfort, but the hope of the future, the life to come. Elijah steps into the chariot of fire, drops his mantle, and is off for that better country. Daniel, in speaking of the future, says, "They that be wise shall shine as the brightness of the firmament: and they that turn many to righteousness as the stars for ever and ever." Nothing in any of these scriptures that, in the remotest sense, even hints at the idea of annihilation or eternal nothingness! All point to something beyond and something better.

Turning to the New Testament, we not only find many allusions to another life, but passages that very directly teach it. Our Lord, to comfort the hearts of his disciples, told them about his Father's house of many mansions, and that he would go away and prepare a place for them; also, that he would come again, and receive them to himself, that where he is there they might be also. Again, he tells them to rejoice and be exceeding glad, for great is their reward in heaven. Then we have the statement, clear and distinct, that Moses and Elias appeared with Christ on the mount. Moses had been dead hundreds of years, and Elias translated nine hundred years, yet there they were alive.

Then we have the case of the rich man and Lazarus, and what Jesus said to the penitent thief, teaching in plain, unambiguous terms the doctrine of a conscious existence after this life. Paul was very positive in his teachings respecting another life: "We *know* that if our earthly house of this tabernacle were dissolved, we have a building of God, an house not made with hands, eternal in the heavens."

Again, he says that to be absent from the body is to be present with the Lord, which, he said, was not only better, but *"far* better." He speaks of things temporal and things eternal-temporal things are seen, eternal things unseen. Stephen saw the heavens opened, and just before he expired, he kneeled down and prayed, "Lord Jesus, receive my spirit." John says, "It doth not yet appear what we shall be: but we know that, when he shall appear, we *shall be like* him; for we shall see him as he is." Peter speaks of "an inheritance incorruptible, and undefiled, and that fadeth not away, reserved in heaven for you, who are kept by the power of God through faith unto salvation." When the vision was opened to John on Patmos, he saw a company before the throne which no man could number. They were from all nations, tongues, and peoples; they were clothed in white robes and sang with a loud voice, "Salvation to our God which sitteth upon the throne, and unto the Lamb." These are but a few of the many passages of Scripture that teach the immortality and future endless existence of man. Add to this the doctrine of the resurrection of the dead, so plainly and clearly taught in the sacred Scriptures, and which stands as proof positive of the immortality and future existence of man, and you have a foundation sufficiently broad and solid upon which to rest your faith, though the heavens fall.

"Though I stoop
Into a dark, tremendous sea of cloud,
Close to my breast, its splendor, soon or late,
Will pierce the gloom: I shall emerge somewhere."

While the Scriptures abundantly teach the certainty of another state of existence, and the endless happiness of the righteous, they just as plainly teach the future endless punishment of the wicked. While the righteous shall enter into the kingdom of God and enjoy the riches of that heavenly inheritance forever and ever, the unrighteous shall go away into everlasting punishment. Nothing unholy or unclean shall ever enter into the kingdom of glory. The pure in heart shall see God. "He that soweth to the Spirit, shall of the Spirit reap life everlasting." "He that soweth to his flesh; shall of the flesh reap corruption." It is right. God is eternally just. The Judge of all the earth will do right.

As a fit closing of this chapter, I will adopt the language of Dr. Thomas Dick: "If we believe that the whole train of circumstances connected with our present lot is arranged by Infinite Wisdom and Benevolence, everything that befalls us here must have a certain bearing on the future world, and have a certain tendency to prepare us for engaging in its exercises and for relishing its enjoyments. In short, if we recognize the fact of an immortal life, we shall endeavor to acquire clear and comprehensive views of its nature, its pleasures, and its employments. We will not rest satisfied with vague and confused conceptions of celestial bliss, but will endeavor to form as precise and definite ideas on this subject as the circumstances of our sublunary station will permit. We will search the oracles of divine revelations, and the discoveries of science, and endeavor to deduce from both the sublimest conception we can form of the glories of that inheritance which is incorruptible, undefiled, and that fadeth not away, which is reserved in heaven for the faithful."

> "It is little matter at what hour of the day
>   The righteous fall asleep. Death cannot come
>   To him untimely who has learned to die.
>   The less of this brief life, the more of heaven;
>   The shorter time, the longer immortality."

The City of God *(page 47)*

"And the city lieth foursquare, and the length is as large as the breadth; and he measured the city with the reed, twelve thousand furlongs. The length and the breadth and the height of it are equal" (Rev. 21:16).

III
HEAVEN — A LOCAL, SUBSTANTIAL PLACE

> "O holy dwelling-place of God!
>   O glorious city all divine!
> Thy streets, by feet of seraphs trod,
>   Shall one glad day be trod by mine."

IT IS A FACT none will care to dispute that we shall be out of this world in a comparatively short time. No matter what our notions or theories concerning the hereafter may be, the edict has gone forth and will not be recalled — "It is appointed unto men once to die." *There is no discharge in this war.* If there is anything beyond this world we should not only know it, but know as much about it as possible. Our present life is transient, there is none abiding; but that beyond is fixed. Is it an eternal sleep or a state of conscious existence? Be it this or that, it is fixed. Of the millions who have gone from us not one has returned to tell us how it is. None have returned for a second trial. The journey once made is made forever.

If there is a question in all the range of human thought about which we ought to be certain, it is that of our future destiny. If it were but for a few short years, it would be far less important; but it is on, on, forever on. A soul saved is saved forever; a soul lost is lost forever. Dean Alford says: "As there is a second and higher life, so there is also a second and deeper death. And as after that life there is no death, so after that death there is no more life!'

> "We shape ourselves the joy or fear
>   Of which the coming life is made,
> And fill our future atmosphere
>   With sunshine or with shade."

As touching the mode of the existence of spirit when separated from the body, we know absolutely nothing. We can only conceive of spirit as we associate it with organization. God is a spirit, but we cannot think of him as such. We think of him as having form, and to accommodate our sense of conception he allows himself to be represented to man as having body and form, otherwise we could not think of him at all. Thus it is with disembodied spirits. We think of them as having form, very similar to what they had on earth. We know it is not thus, yet we cannot think of them otherwise. Inconceivable as spirit-life may be to us now, it must be that the departed spirit carries with it consciousness—the mind thinks right on. Joseph Cook allows that the soul may have "a nonatomic enswathement" when separated from the body. Mr. H. M. Grout thinks that the spirit may have "an ethereal covering, a white raiment," so as to be visible to other beings around it. But who knows what the vision of a disembodied spirit may be? How do we know but that spirit may be able to see spirit? "Now we see through a glass darkly," we see in part, but then we shall see as we are seen. So that spirits in a spiritual realm may see each other without any "enswathement," or "ethereal covering."

Whatever our conceptions respecting the mode of the

existence of the departed spirits may be, we cannot dismiss from our minds the idea of location. Some profess to believe that heaven is simply a state, or condition, and is everywhere in general, and no place in particular. That state, or condition, has much to do in constituting heaven, is not questioned; but that the soul, like a wandering Jew, will go floating about in some "lofty aerial region, mysteriously suspended upon nothing," is not supposable. Things on earth are real, but no more so than they are in heaven. Things on earth are tangible to the senses; so it will be in heaven. The constituent elements of the mind will not be changed in, nor by death. The mind as it is cannot dwell on nothing; it must have something tangible to grasp. So it must always be. Any other conclusion would imply the necessity of a complete reconstruction of the constituent elements of the mind, and virtually destroy the doctrine of immortality and conscious identity. If the mind is not the soul outright, it inheres in it and is inseparable from it. Man is born for a high and noble destiny. He possesses faculties and powers which can be exercised only to a limited extent during a short lifetime. Are these only half-fledged powers to perish forever when man dies? Are reason, memory, and consciousness to fade and die when mortal life ceases? Or, are they to be so completely reconstructed as not to need anything visible or tangible to dwell upon?

Dr. Harbaugh says, "All these faculties are supplied with materials to keep them in life and vigor, through the senses, from an external world."

Shall these faculties be cut off from their sources and conditions and die? If there be nothing visible or tangible in heaven, what use of any of these faculties? Reason cannot dwell upon nothing; it must have something visible or tangible from which to draw analogies.

Heaven, wherever it may be, is a visible, local, material,

substantial place. Those who are accustomed to think of heaven as some sort of an aerial realm will hardly accept with favor the idea of materiality and substantiality. But material things are known to exist in highly refined conditions, such as light and electricity; and for aught we know, matter may exist in a thousandfold higher condition of refinement than either of these. What can we know about materiality in its highest state of refinement, without the taint of sin, and where everything is absolutely perfect? Might not such a place, spiritualized, be suitable for the final home of the saints? Compare such a place with the earth as it now is, all deranged and polluted with sin, where everything, even the most beautiful flower, is tinged and blurred by the withering curse of sin. But this view is not insisted upon; the one purpose in mind is to establish the fact that heaven is a real, substantial place. We cannot think of heaven in any other light. We cannot think of those who have gone from us as floating around in some boundless aerial realm, like homeless wanderers. Such conceptions would almost excite our pity and weaken our aspirations to join them.

Volumes might be written upon the presumptive evidences that heaven is a substantial habitation, but we are thankful that we are not shut up to reason and philosophy alone. Our Heavenly Father has not left us to mere conjecture alone upon a matter of so much importance, the reality of which we must so soon test. No; he has given a revelation which in one way and another teaches the doctrine of a future, visible, tangible home. No one can read this precious Volume without being impressed with the fact that heaven is a real, substantial place. No matter where you locate it, it is a place. Sometimes it is referred to metaphorically, sometimes in general terms, and often specifically. We shall not attempt to give more than a few of the many passages which in one way or another teach the doctrine of a local heaven: "Heaven is my *throne*, and earth is my footstool." "The Lord hath prepared his *throne in the heavens*." "*A glorious high throne*, from the beginning is the *place* of our sanctuary." "Therefore are they before the throne of God, and serve him day and night in his temple." "Blessing, and honour, and glory, and power, be unto him that sitteth upon the throne." Do not scriptures like these suggest the thought that there is some central place in the universe from which the glory of God is reflected in a peculiar manner?

Jesus said to his disciples, and to us as well, "In my Father's house are many mansions." Does not this impress upon the mind the thought of home? Is there a spot on earth more sacred to the heart than home? What fond and tender memories crowd upon each other as we think of father's house—the dear old homestead! But what would home, or father's house, be to us without location or tangibility? So with our Father's house above. How can we think of it as a home without location? Do we, or can we think of it as everywhere in general, and nowhere in particular? This is not, and cannot be so. Dr. Guthrie says: "How sweet is the word *home!* What beautiful and tender associations cluster around it! Compared with it, house, mansion, palace are cold, heartless terms. The thought of it has proved a sevenfold shield to virtue; the very name of it has been a spell to call back the wanderer from the path of vice. Grace sanctifies these lovely affections, and imparts a sacredness to the homes of earth by making them types of heaven. As a home the believer delights to think of it. Thus, when lately bending over a dying saint, and expressing our sorrow to see him lying so low, with the radiant countenance rather of one who had just left heaven than one about to enter, he raised and clasped his hands, and exclaimed in ecstasy, 'I am going home!'" When Philip Phillips, the sweet singer, was near to death, Dr. Talmage wrote him the following letter: "I hear you are going home. I congratulate you. When you get there, kiss for me the sacred hands of Him who was slain to redeem us. When you meet any of my kindred, tell them I expect to join them through the grace that saves the chief of sinners. Cheer up! It will not be a half-second between your pillow and the city of Rapture. As you go in among the choirs of the ransomed to resume your work of Christian song, reserve a seat for me back of the door. Multitudes who were blessed by your singing all around the world will be at the shining gate to welcome you. Good-by! good-by! good-by!" This may appear too realistic for some, but heaven, home, place, are grand realities.

Our Lord told his disciples that he would go away and "prepare a place" for them. That word "place" fixes in the mind the thought of locality. We cannot think of it otherwise. And this is further confirmed when he adds, "I will come again, and receive you unto myself; that *where* I am, there ye may be also." Language could not be more explicit. At another time he said, "Father, I will that they also, whom thou hast given me, be with me where I am; that they may behold my glory, which thou hast given me." Wherever Christ is, there his disciples of all the ages are to be. Where is Christ? He was "carried up into heaven"; "received up into glory"; "is at the right hand of the Father." This is the place of the throne, the heaven of heavens. "Here," says Dr. Dick, "the grandeur of the Deity, the glory of his physical and moral perfections, and the immensity of his empire may strike the mind with more bright effulgence and excite more elevated emotions of admiration and rapture than in any other province of universal nature. In fine, this vast and splendid central universe may constitute that august mansion mentioned in Scripture under the designation of the 'third heaven,' 'the throne of the Eternal,' 'the heaven of heavens,' 'the high and holy place,' and 'the light that is inaccessible and full of glory.'"

Weary, tired one, be of good cheer! Look up and believe; there is a place for you in that far-away home. Jesus has gone to "prepare a place for you"; but he will come again, and receive you to himself. There was where Paul desired to be, which he said is far better.

The saints in their resurrection state will need a substantial dwelling-place. Wonderful as the change in the resurrection may be, the identity of the body will be preserved. Because the resurrection body will be spiritual and immortal some have supposed that it will be spirit. That it will be spiritualized there is no doubt, but that it will be altogether spirit is not, and cannot be true. That is not implied in the idea of a resurrection. The doctrine of the resurrection of the dead as taught throughout the Scriptures carries with it the idea of a visible, substantial body. The resurrection of Christ's identical body as a first-fruit is the assurance of the resurrection of our bodies. Thus the apostle reasons in the fifteenth chapter of First Corinthians.

When Christ appeared to his disciples after his resurrection, they were frightened, supposing it was a spirit. But he calmed their fears by assuring them that it was not a spirit which they saw, but himself: "Behold my hands and my feet, that it is I myself: handle me, and see." Thus in two ways he convinced them, not only that he was the Christ, but that he had the identical body that was crucified and buried. He appeals first to their sight, "Behold my hands and my feet"; then to their touch, "Handle me, and see." He further told them, "A spirit hath not flesh and bones, as ye see me have." In that body "he led them out as far as Bethany;" and after pronouncing upon them his last benediction he was "carried up into heaven." He went to heaven with that same body, visible, tangible, real. With that body he entered heaven, and with that body he appears before the throne as the Lamb of God. In that body he makes intercession for us. Paul says, "We have one mediator between God and men, the man Christ Jesus."

With that same body he will come again, and "every eye shall see him." Now, if heaven is not a substantial place, then the substantial body of Christ that ascended from the presence of the disciples is suspended in nothing, or floating around in some aerial realm, without boundary or stability. But we cannot think thus of our Redeemer. If heaven is only a state, without location, what meaning are we to attach to promises like these: We are to "see him as he is," "be like him," and "with him," and behold his glory?

Respecting the resurrection of the dead, we think it may be helpful in this connection to make a few general statements. Clear views on the cardinal doctrines of Christianity cannot fail to assist us in reaching right conclusions upon final results. The resurrection bodies of the saints will be as real and tangible as the resurrection body of Christ was. There will be a marvelous change—too wonderful for us to understand now. The mortal shall put on immortality, the corruptible shall put on incorruption, and the natural shall put on spiritual. But through all these changes, the identity of the body will be preserved. Dr, Mattison says, "We thus reach the conclusion that *all that constituted or properly belonged to the body at the hour of death, and is essential to its corporal identity,* will be raised again to life, and will go to constitute the new or resurrection body." This conclusion is all the more reasonable when we consider that, when Christ comes, those who shall be living at that time will be *changed,* There will be no difference between the living and the dead. Paul says, "We shall not all sleep, but we shall all be changed, in a moment, in the twinkling of an eye,... this mortal shall have put on immortality."

Another fact should not be overlooked, that during our earth life the body undergoes many changes. Sometimes those changes come very rapidly, but we never lose our identity. The man at seventy years of age is conscious that he is the same person he was at thirty or forty years of age, but he is not conscious that the same particles of matter which composed his body at thirty compose it at seventy. Indeed, he has abundant reason to know that it is not so. What, then, constitutes identity? *Conscious identity is an act of the mind.* Sir William Hamilton says, "Identity is a relation between our cognitions of a thing, not between things themselves." Mr. Locke says every one is to himself what he calls self, without considering whether that self be continued in the same or diverse substances; so that "the personal identity or sameness of a rational being is self-consciousness." In the resurrection the mind will not recognize each particle of the resurrection body as precisely the same that belonged to it at one time or another during its earth life; nor is it necessary that it should do so in order to constitute an identity. The man at seventy years of age does not recognize the particles of matter composing his body as the same that composed it at forty years of age, yet he recognizes his body as his own. So the mortal can put on immortality without destroying conscious identity. The resurrection body, with every imperfection removed, will in form and appearance, be similar to what it now is. I know of no reason why it should not be so. Dr. Harbaugh says: "Heaven could not be a suitable abode for the saints if it were not local, material heaven. The saints will have bodies. Pure spirits may, for aught we know, exist differently; but the saints, having bodies, must have a material dwelling-place because they are material." Because heaven is a material place, and the resurrection bodies of the saints are material, does not in any proper sense detract one iota from the grandeur, beauty, and glory of the place. Materiality, refined, immortalized, and glorified, is far above our highest conceptions of beauty and perfection.

Mr. Knapp says: "According to the New Testament, man will possess a *body*, even in the future life, and continue to be as he now is, a being composed of both *sense* and *reason*; and so there, as well as here, he will have the want of something *cognizable* by the senses." Krummaker says:

"We look for a house, a home—heavenly paternal home—a peopled residence, a real habitation, where we shall know one another and be with one another, upon terms of the most intimate friendship and the dearest fellowship."

Why fritter away such a heaven in our thoughts for some sort of aerial, visionary realm about which we can form no conception? The saints in heaven will be something, not nothing. They will be intelligent and progressive, not idiots. They will not know less, but vastly more than they ever knew on earth. Now they see through a glass darkly, but there they see as they are seen. Now they know in part, but there they shall know as they are known. Now they have glimpses, only glimpses; but there, where the mists are cleared away, they shall see everything in its clearest light. The glory of the Trinity, the glory of heaven, the glory of the angels, and the glory of the whole universe will be open to the view of the saints.

> "Land of the blest, on faith's keen eye
>   Faint glimpses of thy glory break;
> Oh, when in earth's last sleep I lie,
>   Mid thy full splendors let me wake."

Bishop J.W. Hott, D.D., says: "The life of the soul, after it passes the mystery of death, is an instinct of mankind, a hope of pure reason, and a truth of holy revelation. The resurrection and life of the body in some spiritualized form I cherish in hope as a doctrine of the Bible. Heaven is where God is and where the good gather beyond death. I cannot think of the existence of any of these, in any form, without their occupancy of space—place. If it please our Heavenly Father that I exist after death with him, it must be that I shall be somewhere; that is, not everywhere, nor nowhere. So I have come to greatly love the words of Jesus, 'I go to prepare a place for you,' and 'that where I am, ye may be also.' Many very dear to me are now there. I hope for a heaven of vastness of proportion, excellency, and beauty—the crowning work of the great God. If this spiritualized, heavenly dwelling-place may lie within the space about our present world, and other worlds of which we have some knowledge, I shall be glad, and none the less at home. It may embrace the freedom of a large portion of our Father's universe. A little travel and company with God makes the soul at home anywhere. Somehow I think heaven is not far away."

All the representations of heaven that we find scattered here and there throughout the Scriptures, whether they be metaphorical, figurative, or specific, impress the mind with the idea of vastness and location. Abraham is represented as a sojourner in a strange country; but "he looked for a city which hath foundations, whose builder and maker is God." Of his descendants it is said, "God is not ashamed to be called their God: for he hath prepared for them a city." John, on several occasions in his vision from Patmos, had glimpses of the city, and describes it as having gates of pearl, walls of jasper, streets of gold, and a river of life, clear as crystal, flowing through it. What does all this mean? A city of foundations—a city with gates, walls, and streets, and yet no location, no substantial place, no tangibility? That cannot be. Heaven is a place.

Again, the apostle, when speaking of the Israelites, says, "They were strangers and pilgrims on the earth." This they confessed to be; and because they thus confessed, they declared *plainly* that they sought a country—not alone the land of Canaan, for after they had reached that promised land, they desired" a better country, that is, an heavenly." What conceptions have we of a country, be it earthly or heavenly, without location? Did the sacred writers mean to allure by promises which would never be realized? Does God's dealings with his people in past ages warrant us in the belief that he will promise and not fulfill? Why, then, did he put it into the minds of the patriarchs, prophets, and apostles, that there is a better country, a city of foundations, when in fact there is no substantial place—nothing but an aerial realm, in which they might float about forever? It cannot be thus. No, heaven is a veritable place, a real, substantial country.

> "We speak of the realm of the blest
> A country so bright and so fair,
> And oft are its glories confessed,
> But what must it be to be there!
>
> We speak of its pathways of gold,
> Its walks decked with jewels so rare,
> Its wonders and pleasures untold,
> But what must it be to be there!"

Our limits will not permit us to pursue this branch of the subject further. We will close this chapter with a quotation from Dr. Joseph Beaumont: "It is held forth to our view as a *banquet*, where our souls shall be satisfied forevermore; the beauties of Jehovah's face, the mysteries of divine grace, the riches of redeeming love, communion with God and the Lamb, fellowship with the Infinite Father, Son, and Holy Ghost, being the heavenly fullness on which we shall feed. As a *paradise*—a garden of fruits and flowers, on which our spiritual nature and gracious tastes will be regaled. As an *inheritance*, undefiled, and that fadeth not away. As a *kingdom*, whose immunities, felicities, and glories are splendid and vast, permanent and real, quite overwhelming, indeed, to our present feeble imaginings. As a *place*, where dwells the Lord our righteousness, the King in his beauty displayed—his beauty of holiest love; in the eternal sunshine of whose countenance bask and exult the host that worship at his feet. As a *building* that has God for its maker, immortality for its walls, and eternity for its day. As a *sanctuary*, where the thrice divinity enshrined in our nature in the person of Immanuel is worshiped and adored without a sigh, without an imperfection, and without intermission; where hymns of praise, hallelujahs of salvation, and hosannas of redemption, uttered by blest voices without number, ever sound before the throne. As a *temple,* bright with divine glory, filled with the divine presence, streaming with beauty, and peopled with monuments of divine goodness, mercy, and peace."

IV
HEAVEN — VARIOUS THEORIES

WHILE THE RANGE of our natural vision and the realm in which our thoughts may safely ramble are very great, yet they are very far from being boundless. When God gathered the waters together, he fixed their bounds. He "shut up the sea with doors" and said, "Hitherto shalt thou come, but no further: and here shall thy proud waves be stayed." Thus, when God created man and breathed into his nostrils the breath of life and he became a living soul, he fixed a limit to his vision and set bounds for his thoughts. Whenever man attempts to go beyond these bounds unaided by revelation, he enters the field of speculation, and cannot safely affirm anything. What can we know of a world we have not seen, and of which no one has ever informed us?

"The things which are seen are temporal; but the things which are not seen are eternal." O world to come, in exchange for this! O eternity, whatever its condition may be! It is fixed — on, on, forever on; this is temporary — a shadow — "is soon cut off, and we fly away."

Many of the Greek and Roman philosophers reasoned

well on the immortality of man, and sometimes almost affirmed it, yet it is noticeable that here and there between the lines that cheerless word "if" may be found. Having nothing to guide them but their own consciousness, they could not prove the immortality of the soul, and therefore, as philosophers dare not affirm it. While consciousness is not an infallible proof of immortality, it furnishes a strong presumptive evidence that some such thing is true; especially when we consider that it was not only the philosophers that held this opinion, but that all nations, tribes, and peoples, from the remotest antiquity, held the same view. No matter how vague and unreasonable their notions were, they all had their Hesperian gardens, Elysian fields, and Islands of the Blest, located somewhere in the universe, where the souls of the virtuous would dwell forever.

The pagan world, not having any sure word of prophecy to guide them, adopted many strange theories concerning the place and state of the departed. How could they know anything as certain about those who had gone beyond? Who can describe an invisible and unseen world? An astronomer can tell something about the size, distance, and motion of worlds millions of miles away. But who can open the "seven-sealed Book" and see to the end of that "dim, shadowy field, stretching out illimitably before him"? The old philosophers and poets, and, indeed, the whole pagan world, are to be pitied rather than blamed for their vague and superstitious notions concerning an after and better life. "Once in awhile their yearning spirits would attempt to penetrate those dreadful mysteries beyond the line which divides the visible from the invisible, but all their attempts were vain. They were like benighted travelers seeking their way in a dreary wood, bewildered rather than aided by the mimic lights that play around them in the dismal bogs." We who live and walk in the sunlight of God's revealed Word-the one only source of correct and reliable information respecting the life to come—are ill prepared to sympathize with those who have all their lives walked in the shadowy region of ignorance and superstition, seeking another and better life through the gloom which hangs over the grave.

In stating some of the many theories held by the different nations, tribes, and peoples of the world, past and present, I shall not attempt to discuss at any considerable length, either pro or con, the merits or demerits of these several theories. The main purpose in stating them is to show that a belief in the future existence of man is well-nigh universal. No matter how strange and unsatisfactory these notions may appear to us, the fact remains that the belief is as widespread as the race of mankind. Whence this universal opinion? I am free to admit my indebtedness to Thomas Dick, D.D., LL.D., and Rev. H. Harbaugh, D.D., for valuable information obtained from their writings on this far-reaching subject. Only a few of the many theories and notions can be considered in this connection. The natives of the Society Islands, the chiefs of the Friendly Islands, the New Zealanders, the inhabitants of the Pelew Islands, the Kalmuck Tartars, the various tribes of Africa,—the Mandingos, the Jaloffs, the Feloops, the Foulahs the natives of Dahomey,—the Persians, the Japanese, the Wahabee Arabs, and the North American Indians, all believe in the future existence of man. Dr. Dick says, "Among the numerous and diversified tribes that are scattered over the different regions of the earth, that agree in scarcely any other sentiment or article of religious belief, we find the most perfect harmony in their recognition of a Supreme Intelligence, and in their belief that the soul survives the dissolution of its mortal frame." Cicero said, "In everything the consent of all nations is to be accounted the law of nature, and to resist it is to resist the voice of God." In whatever way we may account for the origin and universality of this belief, the fact remains that it inheres in the consciousness of all mankind, and that, too, from the remotest antiquity.

But, while this belief is almost if not altogether universal, there is a wide difference of opinion respecting the *place* and *condition* of departed souls. Some believe in the transmigration of souls; others, that the soul wanders about without any certain dwelling-place; and still others believe that the place and condition of the soul is, and will in many respects be quite similar to what it now is; that the pursuits followed here will be continued there, only under very much better *conditions — always and eternally better.* They also make some distinction between the wise and virtuous, and the ignorant and vicious. Indeed, with but few exceptions, they all hold to the idea of future rewards and punishments in some form or other. "Hence," Dr. Dick says, "it has generally, I might say uniformly, been found that all nations that have acknowledged the existence of a divine Being have likewise recognized the idea of a future state of retribution."

The desire for something better is as universal as the family of man. It is possible to be measurably contented with our lot, but we cannot be satisfied. Long ago one said, "I shall be satisfied, when I awake, with thy likeness." Situated as we are, where nothing is perfect, nothing abiding, it is not surprising that there should be a longing and hoping for something better. With this abiding desire, it is comparatively easy for fancy, in her vision, to picture some far-away home of fadeless beauty and undying pleasure — as an orange grove in some sheltered glen on which the sun is just beginning to shine; trees laden with golden fruit, and balmy with silvery flowers, all at the same time. This is fancy's picture of something better.

Some hold to the theory of progressive ascension — that the soul at death does not go into an abiding-place. "According to this theory," Dr. Harbaugh says, "it has been supposed that the unnumbered worlds which we see rolling through the heavens are the different platforms upon which the successive stages of our spiritual history are to transpire."

This theory suggests to the mind the idea of continual change and progress. It is not a gloomy picture of man's future state, but it lacks confirmation. Nothing in the sacred Scripture warrants any such a belief. "It will easily be seen that this is a refinement of the ancient doctrine of transmigration, and may easily be traced back to that idea as its germ." That the doctrine of endless progression is most reasonable to believe, no thoughtful person will care to controvert; but not by progressive ascensions, as this theory teaches.

Another idea closely allied to this, as given by Mr. Taylor in his physical theory of another life, is that all worlds are divided into two classes—suns and planets. The planets are inferior and subordinate to the suns. The soul at death passes to one or another of these planets, where it is instructed and qualified, and then passes to the sun, and finally to a still higher and more refined state of existence. This is far from being a humiliating theory, and, if we had nothing better to hope for, it would be worth a superhuman effort to gain that final central sun through these successive stages of progressive ascensions. It is infinitely better than that cold, cheerless theory of annihilation, or that long, dreamless sleep in the tomb. But we have something still better to hope for—a country, a home, where neither the light of the sun, moon, or stars will be needed.

> "Beyond these chilly winds and gloomy skies,
>   Beyond death's cloudy portals,
> There is a land where beauty never dies
>   And love becomes immortal;
>
> A land whose light is never dimmed by shade,

Whose fields are ever vernal,
Where nothing beautiful can ever fade,
But bloom for age eternal."

Heaven all about us. This is not a popular theory, nevertheless it has its advocates. The substance of this conjecture is that the planets are like islands of the sea, surrounded on all sides with water, the water representing the spirit-world. This spirit-world surrounding the planets is real, but not visible. It cannot be seen, nor heard, nor felt—a "universe not less real than the one we are at present conversant with; a universe elaborate in structure and replete with life." Neither the one we are conversant with nor this invisible universe has any active affinities—distinct but yet connected. One is sorely puzzled to know upon what philosophical basis such a theory rests. *Invisible, unseen, unheard,* and *unfelt*—how, then, can we know that such a universe exists? We know by a kind of intuition that there is something for man after this life, but where it is or what it is, we cannot tell. We cannot see beyond, and none of our loved ones who have gone from us have returned to tell us how it is; and how can we know? When imagination, untaught, and unaided by a revelation from beyond, attempts to penetrate and explore the invisible realm of spiritual existence, the chances are that it draws many strange and fantastic figures. With all the light we have from nature, reason, and revelation, we cannot describe the mode of spiritual existence. How, then, can a philosopher, however wise he may be, describe it by nature and reason alone? But all these theories and notions, strange as they may appear to us, stand as presumptive proof of the immortality and future existence of man. No matter how vague and unreasonable a theory may be, there are always persons who will advocate it.

Another theory is, in substance, that there is no such place as heaven now, but one will be suddenly created:

"That the visible universe, replete everywhere with various forms of animal life, is to fill one period only in the great history of the moral system, and that it is destined in a moment, in the twinkling of an eye, to disappear and to return to its nihility, giving place to new elements and to new and higher expressions of omnipotence and intelligence." There is nothing horrible or particularly repulsive in this theory, but it is not (like the other theories thus far named) in harmony with the teaching of the Scriptures, nor is there anything in the domain of reason to sustain it. It leaves us in doubt as to the whereabouts of those who have gone from us. Where are they? Are they homeless wanderers having no certain abiding-place? Where are the angels? Where are Enoch and Elijah, who went away bodily? Where is our Lord, who was carried up into heaven from the presence of the disciples? He told them that he would go away and prepare a place for them, and that he would come again and receive them to himself that they might be with him and behold his glory. Jesus Christ was received up into glory, and wherever the glorified form of our Redeemer is there his disciples are to be.

Another theory, and one which has no insignificant number of adherents, is that this earth, when renovated and made every whit pure, will be the future everlasting home of the saints. Many learned and devout men hold this opinion. Arguments from reason and the Scripture are adduced to sustain it; and, like many other theories, there is nothing humiliating or demoralizing in this opinion. The earth, when the curse of sin is all removed and the atmosphere around it purified, would be no mean dwelling-place; but there is still a better country, infinitely better. The scriptures adduced to sustain this view, if taken in a literal sense, would seem to favor it. But the scriptures must be interpreted so as to harmonize with themselves.

The meaning of a text is often to be determined by the connection in which it stands, and by other similar passages found in other and different connections. There are many passages which are to be taken in a metaphorical and not in a literal sense. Thus it is with many passages adduced to prove that this earth, when renovated, is to become the final home of the saints. Dr. Harbaugh says, "The advocates of this strange, out-of-the-way notion are governed rather by the *sound* than by the *sense* of Scripture."

The uniform teaching of the Scripture is that heaven is "above, and far away from this earth. God is 'above.' 'On high.' 'Heaven is my throne, and the earth is my footstool.' 'The Lord hath prepared his throne in the heavens.' 'The throne of the Eternal.' 'The high and holy place.' 'Caught up to the third heaven.' 'Ascended up on high.' In these forms of expression, found throughout the Scripture, we cannot fail to be impressed with the grandeur and magnitude of a place which is the peculiar residence of the Great and Holy One; a vast central empire, exceeding all others in magnitude and splendor, and in which are blended the glories of every system." This is heaven, the third heaven, the heaven of heavens, the home of angels, the throne of God. The earth, when renovated, can never be the capital of the universe. It is quite too small as compared with the dimensions of other known worlds to admit of even a comparison with the vastness of that central empire where the throne of the eternal is.

In our contemplations of that better country our thoughts are not likely to become too exalted. The danger lies in making it too much like earth. The loftier our thoughts of God, the Redeemer, and heaven are, the more deeply will we be impressed with the necessity and importance of a corresponding preparation to dwell in the presence of the High and Holy One. Where the throne of God is, there the glorified form of the Redeemer is; there the angels, cherubim, and seraphim are, and where these are, there the saints are to dwell forever and ever. Their song, as John heard it, will be, "Blessing, and honour, and glory, and power, be unto him that sitteth upon the throne." Now, the idea that the Eternal Father should vacate this central empire, where he has dwelt in inaccessible light and glory through all the eternities, and establish his throne upon this little planet, bringing all the inhabitants of that celestial clime with him, is hardly supposable. Jesus said, "I go to prepare a place for you." He also said, "If I go,... I will come again and receive you unto myself; that where I am, there ye may be also." He did go away, for they saw him when he ascended, and as certainly as he went away he will come again. But where did he go? He told his disciples that he would go to the Father. Now, from the plain words of Jesus, we have these facts: First, that he is with the Father; second, where he is, his disciples are also to be.

The earth is one of the smallest known planets. Dr. Dick says: "The sun is five hundred times larger than the earth and all the other planets and their satellites taken together. On the same scale such a central body as heaven would be five hundred times larger than all the systems and worlds in the universe." Is there not room in the universe for such an empire? If it should please the eternal Father to create and set in motion a thousand worlds as large as the sun every hour for a million years, all beyond would still be a boundless realm of space. We can no more comprehend the vastness of space than we can comprehend the eternity of God. With such thoughts of the universe, the idea that this little earth is to be the central empire, the capital of all worlds and systems, does not comport with our conception of the Deity—of his throne, and the innumerable hosts round and about him.

"While we do not and cannot know where this *place*, this empire, this heaven of heavens is, it is not unreasonable to believe that it is in the center of the universe, around which all worlds revolve in silent but majestic grandeur. "We feel," says Dr. Dick, "oppressed and overwhelmed in endeavoring to form a faint representation of it. But much as it may overpower our feeble conceptions, we ought not to revolt at the idea of so glorious an extension of the works of God, since nothing less magnificent seems suitable to a being of infinite perfections. Our conceptions of the absolute perfections of the Almighty are quite too low if we presume to bring them within the grasp of our limited understanding. The riches of his wisdom and glory are unsearchable, and his ways past finding out. He sitteth upon the throne in that high and holy habitation, from which the grandeur and glory of his physical and moral perfections, and the immensity of his empire may be viewed, and strike the mind with brighter effulgence, and excite more elevated emotions of admiration and rapture than in any other province of universal nature." Some such vision was opened to John when he said: "I saw as it were a sea of glass mingled with fire: and them that had gotten the victory... stand on the sea of glass, having the harps of God," and they sang of Moses and the Lamb, "saying, Great and marvelous are thy works, Lord God Almighty; just and true are thy ways, thou King of saints." This is a most vivid description of the place, the glory, and the employment of the saints in light:

> "They are perfectly blessed, the redeemed and the free,
> Who are resting in joy by the smooth glassy sea;
> They breathed here on earth all their sorrowful sighs,
> And Jesus has kissed all the tears from their eyes.
> They are happy at home; they have learned the new song,
> And warble it sweetly amid the glad throng.
> No faltering voice, no discords are there—
> The melodious praises swell high in the air."

If the future home of the saints, as described in the

Scripture, was only a probability, it would be worth our while not only to cherish, but to cultivate a hope for it. There is something in the thought of such a heaven, both inspiring and uplifting. What is there in the cold, cheerless thought of annihilation, or the eternal sleep of the dead that is uplifting? Is not the thought of an immortal existence, under conditions the most favorable and delightful, infinitely better? Sick, sorrowful, and weary, plodding through life with nothing to hope for but extinction, presents anything but a bright picture of the future. Something within says, "It were just as well not to have been at all, as to cease to be; wherein lies the difference?" But to go through life, rough and rugged, as the way may be, with the hope, yea more, with the assurance of something infinitely better beyond, presents an altogether different picture to the mind.

> "Hope springs eternal in the human breast;
> Man never is, but always to be blest.
> The soul, uneasy and confined from home,
> Rests and expatiates in a life to come."

The Under-world.—Whence am I? Whither bound? Where shall I be? What shall I be? These are old, simple questions, but they are fraught with tremendous interest. In one way or another they have engaged the thought of the wisest, most learned, and devout men of all the ages from the remotest antiquity. A thousand conjectures concerning the future destiny of man have been advanced. When our loved ones go from us, our thoughts, whether we will it or not, follow them. Where have they gone? Have they ceased to be? Do they know anything about us? What have they seen? Are they in the air around us? Have they gone to some far-away realm? Shall I ever see them again? Dr. Harbaugh states it thus: "The spirit of my dear friend who has just now waved me his last earthly farewell, whose tenantless body lies motionless before me, must be somewhere—oh, where? I look around and all is silent. The hearth, the room, the accustomed walks of life—all mourn his absence. I feel as though that form must meet me again which met me before; and, forgetting, I hold my breath and place my finger upon my lips to hear that voice once more, or to be joyfully surprised by his coming footsteps. In the dreadful stillness of the twilight hour I close my eyes, and fancy brings him back, but when I open my eyes the sweet delusion flies away. I look toward the radiant heaven in the starlit hour, and still my heart inquires, Where is that spirit now?"

We may put on the air of a stoic when our loved ones go from us, but deep in the soul there is this question, "I wonder where they are?" We know they have gone from us and cannot return to us. I heard a mother, as she passed out the door of her home following the remains of a lovely daughter, exclaim, "Will she never come back again?" If this were all, the pure, loving heart would break. But it is not all. Hope sings her sweetest song over the graves where sleep the pure and good.

Thus far in the chapter I have given in brief a number of theories concerning the place and state of the departed. I thought it not amiss to give here and there glimpses of the true doctrine, so that we may be able to see how far the Bible theory rises above all other theories. Going back to the earliest ages we shall find that the first ideas of man's future condition were simple, but not well defined. They all believed in the immortality and future existence of the soul, but as to the place and condition of that existence they seem not to have had any clear conceptions. Turning to Job, we find a statement which gives us some idea of their views with respect to the future existence of man: "A land of darkness, as darkness itself; and of the shadow of death, without any order, and where the light is as darkness." The prevailing opinion was that the place of the departed was "a dark, indistinct, and dreamy *under-world.*"

The Hebrew word *Sheol* was used to express their views concerning the state of the dead. The word means, "a region where one sees nothing." To the Hebrews it meant something beyond the grave. The corresponding Greek word, *Hades,* means substantially the same thing—darkness, where nothing is seen. When any other meaning is attached to the word, it must be found in the connection in which it stands. The Hebrews and Greeks, in using the words *Sheol* and *Hades,* mean substantially the same that we do by *eternity.* Of the departed the Hebrew would say, Gone to *Sheol;* the Greek would say, Gone to *Hades;* we would say, Gone to *eternity.* "They signify, in their primary sense, the place of departed spirits, *without any reference at all to their condition as happy or miserable."* The entrance into *Sheol,* the dreary under-world, was supposed to be in the far west, where the sun went down.

As time passed and the people became more enlightened, they had clearer conceptions of the future conditions of the dead. At first they did not have any thought other than that the dead all went to one place, and were all in the same condition. In the time of Josephus, who wrote some fifty years after Christ, the idea of a distinction of character and a separation between the good and the bad in that dark under-world had obtained. It will doubtless be of very great interest to the reader to know just what their ideas were. I will, therefore, give at some length a quotation from Josephus:

> "Now as to *Hades,* wherein the souls of the righteous and unrighteous are detained, it is necessary to speak of it . *Hades* is a place in the world not regularly finished; a subterraneous region, wherein the light of this world does not shine; from which circumstance, that in this region the light does not shine, it cannot be there must be in it perpetual darkness.

This region is alloted [*sic*] as a place of custody for souls, in which angels are appointed as guardians to them, who distribute to them temporary punishment, agreeably to everyone's behavior and manners.

"In this region there is a certain place set apart as a lake of unquenchable fire, whereinto, we suppose, no one hath hitherto been cast, but it is prepared for a day, afore determined by God, in which one righteous sentence shall deservedly be passed upon all men; when the unjust and those that have been disobedient to God, and have given honor to such idols as have been the vain operations of the hands of men as to God himself, shall be adjudged to this everlasting punishment as having been the cause of defilement; while the just shall obtain an incorruptible and never-fading kingdom. These are now, indeed, confined in *Hades*, but not in the same place wherein the just are confined. For there is one descent in this region at whose gate we believe there stands an archangel with a host, which gate when those pass through that are conducted down by the angels appointed over souls, they do not go the same way, but the just are guided to the right hand, and are led with hymns, sung by the angels appointed over that place, unto a region of light, in which the just have dwelt from the beginning of the world not constrained by necessity but ever enjoying the prospect of the good things they see, and rejoicing in the expectation of those new enjoyments which will be peculiar to every one of them, and esteeming those things beyond what we have here; with whom there is no place of toil, no burning heat, no piercing cold, nor any briars there; but the countenance of the Fathers and of the just, which they see always, smiles upon them while they wait for the rest and eternal new life in heaven which is to succeed this region. This place we call the bosom of Abraham.

"But as to the unjust, they are dragged by force to the left hand by the angels allotted for punishment, no longer going with a good will, but as prisoners, driven by violence; to whom are sent the angels appointed over them to reproach them, and threaten them with their terrible looks, and to thrust them still downwards. Now, these angels that are set over these souls drag them into the neighborhood of hell itself; but when they have a near view of this spectacle, as of a terrible and exceeding great prospect of fire, they are struck with a fearful expectation of a future judgment, and in effect punished thereby; not only so, but when they see the place (or choir) of the Fathers and of the just, even hereby are they punished, for a chaos deep and large is fixed between them, insomuch that a just man that hath compassion upon them cannot be admitted, nor can one that is unjust, if he were bold enough to attempt it, pass over it."

Turning from these ancient and unsatisfactory notions concerning the after-life to the New Testament, we cannot help but experience a great relief. Here we find the doctrine of immortality and eternal life set forth without "ifs" or "ands"—no dreamy, shadowy descent into the great unseen—no dark under-world entered from the far west where the sun goes down. No; heaven is set forth as a place, a real, visible, tangible place, full of light and glory; and all who will may enter that realm of peace and delight. Hell is also a place, a region of woe and misery. No one need be in doubt with respect to the future destiny of mankind in general, nor of himself in particular. In the clear light of the Holy Scripture heaven and hell are set forth. They are not together, but separate places. While there may be many inexplicable mysteries connected with man's future existence! all we need to know is made clear and plain.

An Intermediate Place.—There are many modifications

respecting this theory. Purgatory, as held by the Roman Catholic Church, is supposed to be under the earth. Through this region all who finally enter heaven must pass. The wicked who have not believed and been baptized are not permitted to enter purgatory for purification, but go directly to hell. According to this theory none who die are altogether fit for heaven, but are detained for a longer or shorter period to be purified by suffering. The time may be shortened by the prayers and alms of the living. This not only contradicts the plain teaching of God's Word, but detracts from the great doctrine of atonement. It virtually says that Jesus Christ is not able to save to the *uttermost;* that his blood does not and cannot cleanse from all sin and unrighteousness. The saints in heaven are represented as having washed their souls and made them white in the blood of the Lamb—no intimation that they were purified in the flames of purgatory. It is hardly probable that Elijah went to heaven by the way of purgatory, nor did the thief go that way, unless Christ himself went that way. Paul must have been mistaken when he said that to be absent from the body is to be present with the Lord.

Another theory is that this middle, or intermediate, place is a second probation. Dr. Knapp says: "At an early age men were foolish enough to imagine that there is room to obtain an alteration in the yet undecided destiny of departed spirits. In recent years there has been quite a revival of this antiquated theory. The opinion is that men are saved, or may be saved, after death the same as before death. Especially is this probable in the case of the heathen who never heard the gospel in this life. It is supposed that good and evil spirits will be there the same as here, and that good spirits will be able to win some to Christ. As to the heathen, we do not know what God may do for them, but the Scriptures do not warrant us in the belief of a second probation. The whole scheme of human redemption, so far as it is made known to us is directly opposed to any such theory. Turning to the Scriptures we read: "Behold, *now* is the accepted time; behold, *now* is the day of salvation." "The dead praise not the Lord, neither any that go down into silence." "*To-day* if ye will hear his voice, harden not your heart." "The grave cannot praise thee, death cannot celebrate thee: they that go down into the pit cannot hope for thy truth." "I have set before thee *this day* life and death... choose life." From these and many other similar passages the idea of a second probation not only is not implied, but is set aside.

Another phase of this intermediate place is that the souls of the righteous and wicked are detained in separate places until after the resurrection of the body; that neither heaven nor hell is a suitable place for the soul until again united with the body. This opinion is held by a number of learned and devout men. The souls of the righteous are supposed to be in a state of conscious existence, and perfectly happy in their sphere, while the souls of the wicked are in a state of conscious misery. A few passages of scripture have been adduced in proof of this theory, but when taken in their connections it is difficult, if not impossible, to make them harmonize with the general teaching of God's Word. That the righteous may not enter into the full enjoyment of their heavenly place and state until after the reunion of soul and body, is not improbable, but that does not necessarily imply an intermediate place. The redemption of the body from the power and dominion of death is included in the great plan of human salvation; so that when the saints receive their resurrection bodies, changed and fashioned like unto the glorious body of Christ, it may be a source of increased pleasure and delight." To me it seems most reasonable that it should be so.

But turning from all these theories, of which our limits would only allow a brief statement, we very naturally ask, What is the true doctrine concerning the place and state of the departed? Taking the Scripture as our guide, we think the true doctrine, as stated by Dr. Harbaugh, is this: "The saints do immediately enter that place which is called heaven, where the body of the Saviour now is; where the divine manifestations are most clearly and gloriously made; where angels have their proper home, and where all the heirs of Christ shall finally and forevermore be assembled." Paul's idea was that to be absent from the body was to be present with Christ. Wherever Christ is, there the souls of the departed saints are.

Our conception of spirit and spirit life is very limited; and as it relates to their mode of existence, we know nothing at all. That each spirit has a personal, conscious existence must be true; but how they communicate with each other we do not and cannot know. It may be that spirit can see spirit, and thus to the spiritual vision may have form. But, however these things may be, in our thoughts they have form, and must be somewhere. If they are good, we naturally follow them to heaven. Does the mother think of the pure spirit of her babe as being in some unknown and unmentioned world? No; she thinks of it as in heaven and among the angels. We think and speak and sing of our loved ones as being with Christ in that place which he said, "I go to prepare for you."

Our Lord said to the penitent thief, "To-day shalt thou be with me in paradise." The word *paradise*, in its original meaning, signifies a "place inclosed for pleasure and delight." The Greek translators of the Old Testament use the word when they speak of the garden of Eden, but it is used in the New Testament as another name for heaven. Paul was "caught up to the third heaven," — the heaven of heavens, — the place of the divine glory, and the habitation of the blest. But in that same connection he says he was "caught up into paradise." What he calls *heaven* in one place he calls *paradise* in the other, meaning the same thing. This is the paradise — heaven — of which our Lord spoke when he said to the thief, "To-day shalt thou be with me in paradise." They were not in the grave, not in some dark and dreary under-world, but in heaven. Where our Lord went, the forgiven soul of the thief went.

Turning to Revelation, we read that the tree of life is in the midst of the *paradise* of God; that it stands by the side of the river which flows from the throne of God and the Lamb.

Putting these passages together it is very evident that *paradise*, as used in the New Testament, means *heaven* — the place of the throne of God and the Lamb, and the final home of the saints. There is but little difference of opinion as to where Christ now is. He was "carried up into heaven"; "received up into glory." He is with the Father; sitteth at God's right hand. These declarations teach us plainly and positively that Christ is in heaven. Paul said that he desired "to depart, and to be with Christ," which was not only better, but *far better*. He also said that to be absent from the body was to be present with the Lord. To be with Christ is to be in heaven; and to be in heaven is to be with Christ. This is the plain meaning of these scriptures. There are but two places where the saints are said to dwell — "the whole family in heaven and earth"; one family — some in heaven and some on earth. Upon this passage Dr. Clark says, "Believers in the Lord Jesus Christ on earth; the spirits of just men made perfect in a separate state; and all the holy angels in heaven make but one family, of which God is the Father and head."

The Roman Catholic theory is that this family is divided into three parts — one part on earth, one part in purgatory, and the other part in heaven. Others have one part on earth, one part in the air or some intermediate place, the other part in heaven. But Paul did not seem to know anything about a third division or place. "The *whole* family *in heaven* and *earth.*" What an uplifting thought this is to all who know themselves to be members of this family! — God the Father and head, Jesus Christ the elder brother, angels the familiar companions of those in heaven, and ministering spirits to those on earth. Some bright day, when the last member of this family shall have reached home, there will be a reunion in Father's house, such as neither men nor angels ever witnessed. There will be a banquet at which Christ will gird himself and serve them. The beauties of himself, the glory of the Eternal Father manifested through him, the mystery of divine grace, the riches of redeeming love, fellowship with angels and the whole Trinity, will be a heavenly fullness on which the saints will feed and be satisfied forevermore.

Any who may still be in doubt as to whether or not the souls of the righteous go to heaven immediately after the death of the body would do well to read the Book of Revelation through. John had visions of the future *place* and *state* of the redeemed such as no other man on earth ever had. He saw the souls of the departed saints "in heaven," "before the throne of God," "among the angels," "with the Lamb," and many other like glimpses. But he did not see them in purgatory, in the air, nor in any other out-of-the-way place. If Christ is in heaven, and if the angels are there, then the souls of the departed saints are there also.

It often comes to me like an inspiration that sometime I may be there. But what have I ever done to merit such honor and glory? Nothing. If I have ever done anything good, it was only my duty; I merited nothing by it. If I am saved at all, it will be by grace. The song of the saved will be: "Unto him that loved us, and washed us from our sins in his own blood, and hath made us kings and priests unto God and his Father; to him be glory and dominion for ever and ever. Amen." "They that be wise shall shine as the brightness of the firmament; and they that turn many to righteousness as the stars for ever and ever."

"We feel as if a breath might put aside
  The shadowy curtain of the spirit-land,
Revealing all the loved and glorified
  That death hath taken from affection's hand."

V
HEAVEN—A BETTER COUNTRY

> "Beyond these chilly winds and gloomy skies,
>   Beyond death's cloudy portal,
> There is a land where beauty never dies,
>   And love becomes immortal."

THE HOPE FOR SOMETHING better has been the dream of philosophers and poets, pagans and Christians, through all the ages. No matter what opinions men have adopted with respect to the future, it is always better. There is something within, call it by whatever name you please, that aspires for something better. No matter what our environments may be—rich or poor, high or low, sick or well, at home or abroad—all desire something better. No man, be he wise or unwise, can truthfully say, *"I am satisfied."* Contented he may be, but not satisfied. What does all this mean? If man were altogether mortal, would it be thus? Is there not enough in the material world to satisfy the wants of material beings? But give a man half the earth, and the chances are that he would quarrel with the man that owned the other half and demand a resurvey of the boundary lines between them. This desire or aspiration is no more a creature of education than mind is. Each may be cultivated, but neither can be educated into existence. They inhere in us.

One would think that a man like Solomon in all his glory would have been satisfied. But was he? Again and again he exclaimed, "Vanity of vanities, all is vanity." He had riches, honor, and power, as no man on earth had ever had; and yet was no more satisfied than the poorest subject in his kingdom. Again I ask, What does all this mean? Canon Liddon says: "The refusal to be satisfied with the banquet of our earthly life is an honorable discontent; it is the instinct of a being who cannot suppress the promptings of a higher destiny, who even on the threshold of death must look forward and demand a future." Are all these aspirations, longings, and hopes to go down with man to the dreary region of the tomb? Are they all nothing but miserable cheats? Man is not responsible for them, they are part of himself; they inhere in his nature, and he cannot suppress them if he would.

> "If all our hopes and all our fears
>   Were prisoned in life's narrow bounds,
> If travelers through this vale of tears
>   We saw no better world beyond,
>
> Oh, what could check the rising sigh?
>   What earthly thing could pleasure give?
> Oh, who would venture then to die?
>   Oh, who could then endure to live?"

God promised to Abraham, and renewed the promise to Isaac and Jacob, that their descendants should inherit the land of Canaan. Generation after generation, and century after century passed away, but they never lost sight of that

Faith Glimpses *(page 85)*

"But now they desire a better country, that is, an heavenly; wherefore God is not ashamed to be called their God: for he hath prepared for them a city" (Heb. 11:16).

promise. Four hundred years in Egypt and forty years in the wilderness did not destroy that hope. They were all the time longing to enter and possess that goodly land. The time came at last when God, in a most marvelous manner, led them across the Jordan and gave them the long-promised and long-hoped-for country. They ate of its fruit, drank of its water and milk, and tasted its honey. They found it to be just such a country as God had promised. They were out from under the Egyptian lash; they were done with their wanderings in the wilderness; they were now in Canaan, sure enough. But were they satisfied? Paul says they were not, "But now they desire a better country, that is, an heavenly." But they should not be chided for desiring a better country; they could not help it; it was an honorable discontent. There was enough in that goodly land to satisfy all their physical needs; but there were aspirations which sprang like angels from. the temples of their hearts, which they could not suppress, and which nothing in the land of Canaan could satisfy. What were they? They were the longings of immortality, for a realm congenial to the nature of the soul—*something heavenly.* The soul confined in this earthly tenement would gladly fly away to something purer and better. Did not Paul express this sentiment when he said, "For in this [earthly house or tabernacle] we groan, earnestly desiring to be clothed upon with our house which is from heaven"?

That heavenly country is better than this because of its vastness and refined material. By refined material we do not mean material in the sense of corruptibility, but *tangibility*—a real, substantial place, a country, a city, a habitation. If there is anything in the universe of God that is real, it is heaven. We speak of heaven as a spiritual place, and so it is; not spirit in the abstract, but partaking of the nature of spirit; perhaps better expressed by the word *spiritualized.*

Of the vastness of that heavenly empire, mention is made

in another chapter, but we think it well to further consider it in this connection. The purpose of this is to broaden and heighten our thoughts when contemplating the greatness and majesty of the Creator of all things. The place of the throne of the Almighty, who alone comprehends all the eternities, must be in harmony with the dignity and glory of his character. But we have nothing definite to guide us in determining the dimensions of that heavenly place. A few things are written which suggest place. A few things are written which suggest to the mind the idea of vastness. Jesus said, "In my Father's house are many mansions." But of the size and number of these mansions we are not informed. It, however, suggests to the mind the idea of spaciousness. That word *many* may mean billions multiplied by billions. John in his vision saw it as a great city, and describes it thus: "And the city lieth foursquare, and the length is as large as the breadth: and he measured the city with the reed, twelve thousand furlongs. The length and the breadth and the height of it are equal." Upon this text an ingenious writer makes the following calculations: "Twelve thousand furlongs, 7,920,000 feet, which, being cubed, is 496,793,088,000,000,000,000 cubic feet, the half of which we will reserve for the throne of God and the court of heaven, half of the balance for the streets; and the remainder divided by 5,776, the cubical feet in the rooms 19 feet square and 16 feet high, will be almost 21,502,471,000,000,000 rooms. We will now suppose the world always did, and always will contain 900,000,000 inhabitants, and a generation will last 33S! years, and that the world stands 100,000 years—2,700,000,000,000 persons. Then suppose there were 11,230 such worlds, equal to this in number of inhabitants and duration of years, then there would be a room 16 feet long and 17 feet wide and 15 feet high for each person, and yet there would be room."

Now, while this calculation may be mathematically correct, it is nevertheless largely speculative; and yet not wholly so, for John gives a basis which very naturally sets the imagination to work. "He measured the city with the reed, twelve thousand furlongs. The length and the breadth and the height of it are equal." I presume the measurement was correct, and no matter how we may calculate it we cannot divorce from our thoughts the idea of vastness. To our mortal eye this earth is a large world, but when compared with the size of other known worlds it diminishes into a small affair. According to astronomical measurement we learn that Jupiter is more than twelve hundred times greater in volume than the earth, and Herschel, or Uranus, is seventy-four times larger than our globe. The sun, the great master-wheel of the solar system, is one million two hundred and fifty-three thousand times larger than the earth. It is not at this day considered any very great feat to circumnavigate the earth, but if one should undertake to go around a world as large as the sun, starting when young, he would be older than Methuselah by the time he completed the journey. Is it supposable that the Father of the universe, to whom all worlds belong, and who alone has the right to occupy the boundless realm of space, would dwell in a central empire smaller than the worlds around him? It is not unreasonable to believe that the place of the eternal throne, where the glory of the Trinity is manifested, and where the angels and all the higher order of intelligences dwell, should be larger and grander than any of the worlds which revolve around it. But if heaven is no larger than the sun, it would be more than twelve hundred thousand times as large as the earth. But it is not overtaxing the imagination to allow that heaven is as many times larger than the sun as the sun is larger than the earth.

"Large are the mansions in my Father's dwelling;
　Glad are the homes that sorrow never dims;
　Sweet are the harps in holy music swelling;
　　Soft are the tones that raise the heavenly hymn."

Heaven Composed of Better Material—The earth is not what it was when the Creator pronounced it not only good, but very good. Everything in and around the earth was pure then, but sin has made sad havoc with this once beautiful world. A few things remain to remind us of its former beauty and value—gold, silver, precious stones, flowers, foliage, and fruits. But none of these are perfect. Sin has tainted and polluted everything. The earth upon which we walk, the water we drink, the fruits we eat, and the air we breathe, are all poisoned with sin. The name of death is written upon every living thing. Decay and dissolution is stamped upon everything—nothing pure, nothing substantial. Dr. Cummings says: "Sin defiles the earth to its every acre. Its foul, foul trail may be traced from Paradise in ruins onward to the uttermost end of the globe. There is no spot it has not breathed on. There is no flower it has not blasted. There is no beautiful scene it has not tarnished and spoiled by its pestilential presence. Disloyalty to God is the fever that now agitates creation." But the earth with all its works shall be burned up, and the elements melted with fervent heat. But the heaven of heavens, the place of the throne, the dwelling-place of angels and the final home of the saints, will remain forever and ever.

Of the material of that better country we have but imperfect conceptions. We have never seen a perfect thing. Our vision is so blurred and dimmed by sin that if a perfect object were presented to us we could not see its perfection. We know that heaven is pure, and the material imperishable—the purest of the pure and the fairest of the fair. While it will not be spirit, it will partake of the nature of spirit. It will be visible, tangible, and real. Every saint in heaven will have a body as real as he has on earth, but it will be changed and fashioned like unto the glorious body of the Redeemer. It will not be spirit, but spiritualized. The resurrection body, though spiritualized, will be a body still; so heaven, although composed of spiritualized material, will be a substantial place.

John saw that heavenly country, and in one of his descriptions of it says that it is a great city. Of the dimensions of this city we have spoken, but we wish now to consider the material of which it is composed. He says that the walls of the city had "twelve foundations," and were "garnished with all manner of precious stones" — "jasper," "sapphire," "chalcedony," "emerald," "sardonyx," "sardius," "chrysolyte," "beryl," "topaz," "chrysoprasus," "jacinth," "amethyst." The walls were of "jasper," and the city had twelve gates; and "every several gate was of one pearl: and the street of the city was pure gold, as it were transparent." Through this beautiful city flows the river of life, clear as crystal. If this is figurative language it nevertheless has an allusion to heaven, for the revelator immediately adds: "I saw no temple therein: for the Lord God Almighty and the Lamb are the temple of it," and the "glory of God did lighten it, and the Lamb is the light thereof." Abraham "looked for a city which hath *foundations,* whose builder and maker is God." The patriarchs all looked toward such a city — something that would abide. So there is something more than a mere figure in this language.

From this description of heaven we can hardly fail to be impressed with two thoughts — first, that heaven is real, a substantial habitation, a city of "foundations"; second, that it is composed of the finest and purest material. "As a city," says Dr. Beaumont, "whose walls are burnished gold, whose pavements are jasper, sardonyx, and onyx, through which flows the river of life; the inhabitants of which hunger no more, thirst no more, die no more. As a country whose wide regions we shall traverse in all the might of our untried faculties, and in all the glow of new and heaven-born energies, discovering and gathering fresh harvests of intelligences, satisfaction, and delight."

Toward this better country, this city of foundations, the

patriarchs looked and confessed that they were strangers and sojourners on earth; that here they had no abiding-place, no city of foundations, but they sought one to come. Thus it is with Christians to-day. All are pilgrims and way-farers. That word "pilgrim" is tender and significant. It is not so much the dress that makes the pilgrim, as the heart. The king in royal robes and the beggar in rags each have a pilgrim's heart. They may each have a title to a home in that heavenly city. Who that passed by Lazarus at the rich man's gate would have thought that under his rags and scars he had a genuine pilgrim's heart, with a title, properly recorded in the home office on high, to an inheritance, an abiding-place in that far-away city of God? They buried him in the potter's field—no, they buried his rags, but he, in company with the angels, had gone home.

Christian pilgrim, look up, be of good cheer, contemplate the destiny that lies before you! It is no dream, no delusion, no wild fancy, but a blessed reality. It rests upon the promise of God, which is a thousand times firmer than the earth and heavens. These may pass away, but the promises will abide. Think of the vastness of that heavenly country to which you are going, the central empire of the universe, millions and millions of times larger than the earth. Think of it as composed of the finest material, every thing absolutely perfect. In this sinless realm, and with sinless beings, you are to dwell forever and ever. Think of walking without weariness in the light of the throne of God and the Lamb; walking with loved ones among the evergreen trees that stand on the banks of that beautiful river, and ever and anon meeting with such as Abraham, Moses, David, the prophets, and the apostles. This, my beloved, is to be your home.

> "Out of the shadow of sadness
> Into the sunshine of gladness,
>   Into the light of the blest;

Out of a land very dreary,
Out of the world of the weary,
   Into the rapture of rest.

"Out of to-day's sin and sorrow
Into the blissful to-morrow,
   Into a day without gloom;
Out of a land filled with sighing,
Land of the dead and the dying,
   Into a land without tomb.

"Out of a life of commotion,
Tempest-swept oft as the ocean,
   Dark as the wreck drifting o'er,
Into a land calm and quiet,
Never a storm cometh nigh it,
   Never a wreck on its shore,"

VI
HEAVEN — PROGRESS AND EMPLOYMENT

"For such the bounteous providence of Heaven,
In every heart implanting the desire
Of objects new and strange to urge us on
With unremitted labor to pursue
Those sacred stories that await the ripening soul
In Truth's exhaustless bosom."

WHATEVER OPINIONS WE MAY have adopted concerning man, physically, mentally, and morally, we find in him capabilities for making advancement toward perfection. We find also that he is never satisfied with that to which he has attained. Progress seems to be the law of the mind. The farther he goes, the more ardent are his desires to go still farther. As he ascends in the scale of intellectual knowledge the field for improvement both lengthens and broadens; the more he learns, the more he sees there remains to be learned. This is the experience of the wisest and best men that live, or ever did live.

Sir Isaac Newton, notwithstanding his marvelous attainments, said, "I feel like a child on the seashore gathering up pebbles, while the great ocean lies before me unexplored." This cannot be said of the brutes. In their native state, untutored by man, they are about the same as they always were. The birds build their nests and the bees construct their cells just as they did a thousand years ago—no evidence of progress or any desire for improvement. In a comparatively short time a brute "has all the endowments he is capable of, and were he to live ten thousand years would be the same thing he is at present." But is it thus with man? Let the history of the present century, now about to close, speak. The brute lives in the same world, with the same environments as man, and yet he plods along as did his kind a thousand years ago. But not so with man, for up to the latest period of his earth-life there remains the capabilities, joined with the ardent desire for acquiring new accessions of knowledge. Whether it is in the intellectual or the moral realm, man is never happier than when he is progressing—going forward and upward.

> "Say, can a soul possessed
> Of such extensive, deep, tremendous powers
> Enlarging still, be but a finer breath
> Of spirits dancing through their tubes awhile,
> And then forever lost in vacant air?"

"There is not, in my opinion," says a celebrated essayist, "a more pleasing and triumphant consideration in religion than this of the perpetual progress which the soul makes toward the perfection of its nature, without ever arriving at a period in it. To look upon the soul as going on from strength to strength, to consider that she is to shine forever, with new accessions of glory, and brighten to all eternity, that she will still be adding virtue to virtue and knowledge to knowledge, carries in it something wonderfully agreeable to that ambition which is natural to the mind of man. Nay, it must be a prospect pleasing to God himself to see his creation forever beautifying in his eyes, and drawing nearer to him by greater degrees of resemblance."

Nothing is, or can be more reasonable than the endless progress of the human mind. If the mind, or soul, survives the dissolution of the body, which reason, consciousness, and revelation say it does, then to be happy it must progress. Such are the elements, attributes, or powers of the mind that it can neither be happy nor contented without progression. Take man in his earth-life, and we find in him an ardent desire for increased and increasing knowledge. Then, we are to consider the ample provisions the wise and benevolent Creator has made for the contemplation and improvement of the intellectual and moral powers of the mind. In the vast field thrown open before the mind there seems to be no limit. When I first commenced the study of the Scriptures, it seemed to me that it would not take long to master all there was in them. But now, after sixty years' experience, I find myself much farther from the end than I supposed I was when I commenced.

What astonishing strides the astronomers, philosophers, and scientists have made within the last few centuries! New discoveries and new inventions have been the order of the day. All this has taken place under the most unfavorable conditions. Every inlet and outlet through which the mind operates and communes with other things is imperfect. The eyes are blurred, the ears are dull, and the brain heavy and disordered. But in spite of all these hindrances and disadvantages the mind has advanced. Laws and forces which for centuries were hidden away have been discovered, and many of them utilized and made servants to man. New worlds, and whole systems of worlds, have been discovered. It has been ascertained that within the limits of the system of which our little earth forms a part, there are twenty-nine planetary bodies which contain a mass of matter more than four hundred and twenty-two times greater than the earth; besides the numerous comets, which are traversing the planetary regions in all directions, and the immense *globe* of the *sun,* which is like a universe in itself, and which is seven hundred and fifty times larger than the earth and all the planets and comets together. The size, motion, and grooves along which these vast bodies move have been reduced to almost a mathematical certainty. And still the mind goes on with every increasing desire for something higher and better.

But, take a survey of our immediate surroundings, and see what the human mind hath wrought. Some may doubt what the astronomers say concerning the heavenly bodies, but let us contemplate what has been accomplished immediately around us, and which we cannot question. Consider the improved and increased machinery, with the application of nature's forces to keep it in motion. Look at the utilization of steam, electricity, and gas; the engineering of railroads up and down the mountain slopes; the uses which have been made of iron-ore, from the fine and delicate hair-spring in a watch to the massive structure of bridges and immense buildings. All this, and a thousand times more, has been wrought out by the human mind, and still it goes on and on, gathering strength and power as it goes. Every once in a while some one stops long enough to take a long breath and ask, "What next? Have we not reached the end?" "Spain once held both sides of the Mediterranean at the Strait of Gibraltar. So highly did she value her possessions that she stamped upon her coin the two Pillars of Hercules (as the promontories of rock were called); and on a scroll thrown over them there were the words *ne plus ultra*— no more beyond. But one day a bold spirit sailed far beyond these pillars and found a new world of beauty. Then Spain, wisely convinced of her ignorance, struck the word *ne* from the coin and left *plus ultra*— more beyond. How many a man, whose conceit is great, thinks he has reached the limits of knowledge, when further investigation would open to him a continent of truth before unknown."

While progress is the law of the mind, it is, and of necessity must be, gradual. Whatever grows is gradual. A tree does not spring from an acorn to a sturdy oak in a day; the grain of corn planted in the ground does not appear in the full ripe ear in an hour. So with the unfolding of the mind. No one can go from the lower to the upper round of the ladder of knowledge in a single bound. The trembling of a lid on a teakettle is a very different thing from an engine on the track drawing a train of cars and moving at the rate of forty miles an hour; yet from the former the mind, by gradual steps, reached the latter. Thus it is in all departments, grand ideas and results are reached by successive steps and in no other way. The elder Herschel discovered a planet which he fancied to be the very outpost or corner of the universe. But later the younger Herschel discovered one far beyond, and, it is said, wept because his father was not there to see it. So, in whatever direction we turn our thoughts, whether it be in the physical, mental, or moral universe, we shall find that beyond the limits where our investigations have carried us, there are vast fields which we have not entered, and which we will not have the time nor the ability to enter during our short stay on earth. Then it is to be remembered that whatever progress the mind makes while on earth is made under very great difficulties. We must study in the twilight, in the midst of smoke, and dust, and mist, where at best we can only "see through a glass, darkly."

If, under these most unfavorable conditions, the mind progresses in knowledge, and we know to a certainty that it does, what may we not expect from the same mind under thousandfold better conditions? Some are of the opinion that the moment a soul enters heaven it will know all that it ever will know. But this is contrary to all the known laws governing mind in this life, and unless there shall be a complete reorganization of all the powers of the mind, it cannot be true in heaven. Intelligence, reason, memory, and consciousness are faculties of the mind here, and always will be, unless conscious identity and individuality shall cease to exist. That mind possessed of such tremendous powers should suddenly cease to advance in knowledge, or cease to be altogether, is neither reasonable nor desirable. Cicero said, "When I consider the wonderful activity of the mind, so great a memory of what is past, and such a capacity of penetrating into the future; when I behold such a number of arts and sciences, and such a multitude of discoveries thence arising, I believe, and am firmly persuaded that a nature which contains so many things within itself cannot be mortal."

Rev. H. H. Fout says: "The inspiration of the present life, with its imperfect environments, is the assurance that its sunset gates mark the limit of the embarrassing control of material laws, and open into a realm of larger life, growth, and destiny, where the buds of noble aspirations blossom in heavenly beauty. Immortality is not a satisfying thought apart from the idea of progression. Man is conscious of the capacity of his powers for infinite advancement, and eternity is required for the unfolding of the soul's possibilities. Progress and happiness are inseparable. The happy results of heaven's employment will be eternal progression in knowledge and higher expressions of the divine image."

There will be a very great difference between progress in this life and progress in the life to come. But all the difference will be in favor of the life in heaven. Every step we take forward and upward while here is attended with more or less anxiety, toil, or weariness, but there it will be with ever-increasing delight and pleasure. Here we walk and think and work amid the dying and the dead, but no deaths nor troubles will be in heaven. Here it is half day and half night, but no night shall be in heaven. Here we encounter many things that hinder our progress,— sickness, sorrow, temptations, disappointments, losses, and bereavements,— but there no grief will stir the heart, no tear of sorrow fall, no word of unkindness be spoken, no sighs of suffering heard, no discord disturb the blessed harmonies of the saints or angels. Progress under such conditions will be exceedingly delightful.

> "We speak of its pathways of gold,
>   Its walls decked with jewels so rare,
> Its wonders and pleasures untold,
>   But what must it be to be there!"

The saints in that heavenly realm will be in a condition to advance in knowledge as they could not do while on earth. All bodily infirmities will be removed and the environments will be all that an immortal mind could desire. Whether knowledge will be acquired by a process of study, or come gradually by intuition, we may not know, but in either case it will be attended with the most exquisite delight and pleasure. Solomon says that "much study is a weariness to the flesh," but it will not be thus in heaven. However active the mind may be, when clothed with immortality it will never be heard to say, "I am tired."

It may be well in this connection to note that while the vision of the saints will be clearer and more far-reaching in heaven than it can be on earth, and while they may, and doubtless will be in a condition to move more rapidly there than here, they will not be omnipresent. There will be a limit to their vision and presence. God only is omniscient and omnipresent. The geography of heaven will doubtless be studied. Concerning its vastness, as elsewhere stated, we have no definite information. Hints dropped here and there through the Scriptures impress the mind with the thought of vastness. Allowing it to be the central empire of the universe, it is certainly not unreasonable to believe that it is equal in dimensions to any of the worlds around it. Suppose it is no larger than the sun, it would then be more than twelve hundred thousand times as large as this earth. The study of the geography of such a country will be no small affair, especially when we remember that its history runs back through all the eternities. Then it is hardly to be supposed that such an extensive empire is one continuous plain, with nothing but everlasting sameness everywhere. It is only reasonable to believe that there is, and always will be an endless variety in the scenery and objects to admire in that better country. It will not likely be less varied than the earth. Cursed and polluted by sin as this world is, yet it affords an almost endless variety. There are not two acres of ground, nor two objects, however small they may be, which are exactly alike. Will heaven be less varied than the earth? We cannot think of different localities in a great city nor in a vast country as precisely the same in every particular.

Then, the saints will have presented to their view worlds and systems of worlds. The history, motion, geography, geology, and mineralogy of all these worlds will be studied. But will the saints in light be interested in matters of this sort? Why not? Will they be less intelligent in their heavenly state than they are now? As the history of those worlds is unfolded to the view and understanding of the saints it will be an intellectual feast. How the wisdom, power, and goodness of the eternal Father will shine out from all these sources! Paul reckons that the suffering of this life, whatever it may be, is not even "worthy to be compared with the glory which shall be revealed to us-ward." In another place he speaks of it as an "eternal weight of glory." As the mind progresses along these heavenly paths of knowledge there will be increased and increasing delight. The path of the pilgrim saint on earth is represented as shining more and more as he advances; so I think it will be in heaven. Brighter and brighter, brighter and brighter—on, forever on!

There have been, and now are, astronomers who, if they had it, would give millions of dollars to know what cannot be known on earth concerning the planetary system. Will the minds of such men cease to be interested in the marvelous works of the Creator now that all hindrances are removed, and they can go out on mental excursions and know to a certainty what they could not know while on earth? John, from his island home, had a glimpse of the saints in light. He saw them standing on what appeared like a sea of glass mingled with fire, and he heard them sing, saying, "Great and marvellous are thy works, Lord God Almighty; just and true are thy ways, thou King of saints." This is a glowing description both of the place and employment of the saints in their heavenly home. With visions bright and clear they look out over the mighty universe and see world balancing world, system balancing system, all moving with military precision in silent grandeur around each other, and at a speed that utterly bewilders our earthly senses.

God is not indifferent about his works. Hear him as he speaks to Job: "Canst thou bind the sweet influences of Pleiades, or loose the bands of Orion? Canst thou bring forth Mazzaroth in his season? or canst thou guide Arcturus with his sons? Knowest thou the ordinances of heaven? canst thou set the dominion thereof in the earth?" Astronomers know something about the planetary system, but which of them can tell us all about the "ordinances of heaven"? Are the saints never to know more about the order, motion, number, and magnitude of the heavenly bodies than now? Is it not more reasonable to believe that the great and good Father would give his children an opportunity, under more favorable conditions, to study and become better acquainted with the "ordinances of heaven"?

It is a fact beyond all controversy that man is endowed with intellectual faculties which are susceptible of very great improvement. To what degree of perfection the faculties may be carried, we cannot know. It is also a fact that mortal life is too short and the conditions too unfavorable for even an approximate development of these powers. Is it reasonable to believe that an infinitely wise and benevolent Father would create and endow man with such powers and then forever withhold from him the opportunity of using them? That cannot be. God has provided some better things for those who will accept them. In the life to come there will be ample scope for the fullest exercise of all the intellectual powers of man. Standing on that sea of glass which is doubtless a representation of the glory of the place, they, with unclouded mind and clearest vision, will be able to penetrate, and step by step to understand the plans and operations of the divine mind in the creation and movements of the heavenly bodies.

But man is endowed not only with intellectual faculties, but with moral powers as well. There are "interwoven in his constitution powers, principles, instincts, feelings, and affections, which have a reference to his improvement in virtue, and excite him to promote the happiness of others." The powers, like the intellectual faculties, are susceptible of vast improvement. But life is too short for their full development. It will take an eternity of active, progressive existence to bring them to their full expansion. The perfection of the attributes of God, the work of creation, the scheme of human redemption, and the glory of his providences, are but imperfectly understood by the saints on earth. These are subjects upon which the mind, in the clearer light of heaven, will dwell with ever-increasing delight. The psalmist felt oppressed when he contemplated the greatness of the Creator. "Such knowledge is too wonderful for me," and his "ways past finding out." Paul felt impressed in a similar manner when he exclaimed: "Oh the depth of the riches both of the wisdom and knowledge of God! how unsearchable are his judgments, and his ways past finding out." There will be ample scope in heaven for the full exercise of all the powers of the saints in light. They may ascend, as on an inclined plane, forever and ever, and yet not attain to the perfections of him" whose ways are past finding out."

President Asa Mahan, D.D., says: "It is not probable that such mental and moral powers as our Creator has given us will lie inactive through eternity. The most sublime feature in the human mind is its law of unlimited progression. Place it under circumstances favorable for development and there is no limit to its onward progress. Verily, such minds were made for heaven— where we come into perfect sympathy with the Infinite Mind and where both mental and moral will be eternally active, and where, consequently, such attainments as angels have reached will be our perfect blessedness."

Activity is as much the law of the mind as progression. They mutually imply each other. While the mind will be employed m the study of great problems, there will be other fields which will require active service. There will be something in heaven to do. The whole Trinity is active, angels are active, and so the saints will be. The idea of entering heaven and sitting down in some quiet nook or corner, and thus while away the unnumbered ages of eternity, is not to be thought of. Both the intellectual and moral powers of man revolt at such a theory. These are all made for action, and find their greatest pleasure when in full and free activity. Our Lord said, "My Father worketh hitherto, and I work." But, however active the saints in light may be, it will all be without weariness or fatigue. Again and again have the angels visited this world, teaching us that activity is the order among the inhabitants of heaven. In the resurrection state the saints are to be "equal to the angels," and it is hardly to be supposed that they will be less active than they.

Our knowledge of the universe is so limited that we cannot at present form any just conceptions of its magnitude. It is hardly supposable that the worlds within our view comprise the whole of creation; neither is it probable that this little earth is the only world our Father has peopled with intelligent beings. For aught we know, and reason would sustain the thought, there are millions of worlds beyond the reach of the astronomer's most powerful instrument, and many of these worlds may be peopled with intelligent beings. Taking the most conservative view of the vastness of the universe, we can hardly fail to be impressed with the thought that the scope for the study, progress, and activity of both saints and angels will be ample and complete. Furthermore, we are not at all certain that the work of creation is ended. If it should please the Almighty Father, he could create and set in motion millions of worlds and systems of worlds, and still beyond all these would remain that boundless realm of space. O ye saints of the Most High God, as you wearily plod along life's rugged pathway, look up! there is a destiny lying open before you, the very thought of which ought to thrill your souls through and through.

> "Can man conceive beyond what God can do?
> Nothing but quite impossible is hard.
> He summons into being with like ease
> A whole creation and a single grain.
> Speaks he the word? a thousand worlds are born.
> A thousand worlds? There's space for millions more.
> And in what space can his great Fiat fail?
> Condemn me not, cold critic, but indulge
> The warm imagination. Why condemn?

> Why not indulge such thoughts, as well as our hearts,
> With fuller admiration of that Power
> Which gives our hearts such high thoughts to swell?
> Why not indulge in his augmented praise?
> Darts not his glory a still brighter ray?
> The less is left of chance and the realms
> Of hideous night."

From heaven, the central empire of the universe, "embassies may be occasionally dispatched to all surrounding worlds in every region of space. Here, too, departments from all the different provinces of creation may occasionally assemble, and the inhabitants of different worlds mingle with each other, and learn the grand outlines of those physical operations and moral transactions which have taken place in their respective spheres. Here may be exhibited to the view of unnumbered multitudes objects of sublimity and glory which are nowhere else to be found within the wide extent of creation."

There may, and doubtless will be, errands of love and mercy to perform; messages to be carried from world to world, such as the angels have once and again brought to this world. God could carry on the affairs of his government without the employment of angels, but that is not our loving Father's way. He will have something for his children to do, — not for his sake alone, but for their's as well, — and with what eager delight his commands will be obeyed. From the manner in which the angels announced the birth of Christ to the shepherds, we cannot think that they were otherwise than delighted with the message they were sent to deliver. Paul says that angels are ministering spirits sent forth to minister to the heirs of salvation. Mention is made in many places throughout the Holy Scriptures of the frequent visitations of angels. Then Moses and Elias visited and talked with Christ on the mount. In like manner, the saints and angels from around the throne may

Gathering Home *(page 107)*

"And they shall come from the east, and from the west, and from the north, and from the south, and shall sit down in the kingdom of God" (Luke 13:29).

be sent out with messages of love and mercy to the inhabitants of other worlds.

But some one may say that this picture is overdrawn. No, the chances are that it is underdrawn. I could not draw a picture that would even approximate the grandeur and glory of the place and state of the saints of the living God. Let us stop a moment and note a few facts: (1) The saints are to be like Christ. (2) They are to be equal unto the angels. (3) They are to see as they are seen. (4) They are to know as they are known. (5) They are to shine like suns and stars. (6) They are to be kings and priests. (7) They are to be all immortal and glorified. (8) They are to be crowned with crowns of righteousness. Add to this John's description of the heavenly city, which is to be the final home of these saints, and then tell me if it is possible to overdraw a picture of such a scene.

Pilgrim sojourner, be of good cheer! Look up and believe that some day, not, maybe, so far hence, you will enter into that better country, into that delightful summer land where you will have ample time and scope to enjoy all and a thousand times more than you can now anticipate. Some one said, "Blessed are they that are homesick, for they shall come to their Father's house."

> "But, though earth's fairest blossoms die,
>   And all beneath the skies is vain,
> There is a brighter world on high,
>   Beyond the reach of care and pain."

VII
HEAVEN—SOCIETY, RECOGNITION

> "Blest be the tie that binds
>   Our hearts in Christian love;
> The fellowship of kindred minds
>   Is like to that above."

SOCIETY, IN ITSELF considered, is a necessity. Man is formed for society, and when in his normal condition can neither be happy nor contented without it. It inheres in the mind rather than in the body. When God created man he endued him with a social element; hence he said, "It is not good that the man should be alone." If these social elements in man are not abused, but properly cultivated and developed, they will become a source of great happiness and profit. Unity is an essential element of good society. "Behold, how good and how pleasant it is for brethren to dwell together in unity!" Confidence, kindness, and sympathy always inhere in good society. But sin has ruined everything, so that human society on earth, at its very best, is only an imitation of what God intended that it should be. Society among men is so divided and subdivided that it resembles cliques, rather than society proper. In these divisions character is not always made a test of membership. Wealth, position, and gain are often made the only considerations, while everything else is made subordinate. Numerous societies, both open and secret, are formed for various purposes, some of which are good and some evil in their tendency. But it is not of these divisions and subdivisions in society that I wish to speak particularly, but of society in general.

Strictly speaking, the inhabitants of the whole member of this society holds something in common with every other member. God "hath made of one blood all nations of men," and but for the evil consequences of sin we have reason to believe that one common interest would govern the whole family of mankind. But sin has so demoralized man that selfishness is more nearly universal than philanthrophy [sic]. A proper recognition of the fatherhood of God and the brotherhood of man would change the whole order of things in human society. A lawyer asked our Lord, "Who is my neighbour"? How beautifully Jesus answered him by giving the case of the good Samaritan and the wounded Jew. Our neighbor is not simply the one that lives near by us; but he who comes near to us, even from a distant country, has a claim upon us. Any person we know, or hear of, or pass by, is our neighbor and is entitled to our sympathy and aid if in need or distress. The priest and Levite passed by on the other side, but the Samaritan stopped and gave relief. After thus stating the case, Jesus turned to the lawyer and asked, "Which now of these three, thinkest thou, was neighbour unto him that fell among the thieves?" The lawyer answered, "He that showed mercy on him." Then our Lord said, "Go, and do thou likewise." Is not this as it ought to be? And does it not teach us the doctrine of the universal brotherhood of man?

While human society is not utterly bad, there are so many evil things in it that we can hardly appreciate the good there may be. There is the piteous cry of woe and distress coming from all lands and all the people of the earth. We have the millionaires, the aristocrats, the tyrants, and the beggar all in the same community. Then we have the thief, the murderer, the robber, and the libertine all around us. We pass them on the streets, sit with them in the same car, stop with them at the same hotel, register our names in the same book, and eat at the same table. We never know when nor where we are safe. Dr. Cummings says: "Society at present is full of uncertainty and misapprehensions; its best circles are pervaded by suspicions. No man has perfect confidence at all times in his brother. The face is not always the exact exponent of the heart. The word is not always the true echo of the thought. Man often seems to his brother what he is not, and is often what he seems not to be." "Am I my brother's keeper?" has come ringing down through the ages from wicked Cain until now. How few, comparatively, have practically adopted the doctrine of the universal brotherhood of mankind.

With comparatively few exceptions man is for himself. Turning our thought to the past we behold a "scene of perfidy, avarice, and injustice and revenge,—of wars, rapine, devastation, and bloodshed; nation rising against nation, one empire dashing against another, tyrants exercising the most horrid cruelties, superstition and idolatry immolating millions of victims, and a set of desperate villians [sic] termed *heroes* prowling over the world turning fruitful fields into a wilderness, burning towns and villages, plundering palaces and temples, drenching the earth with human gore, and erecting thrones on the ruins of nations." This is only a glimpse of the past. Age after age the same state of things continued until millions upon millions were swept from the earth.

But the history of the past does not stand alone. Ever

and anon history repeats itself. What are some of the scenes of the present century? Are they not on a par with the long ago? Bloodshed and carnage, confusion and malevolence, vice and cruelty, triumph over virtue, peace, and righteousness. Look at the avaricious, and the loose measures they often employ to gain wealth. Observe the unnatural jealousies between those of the same profession, between husbands and wives, parents and children, brothers and sisters. Then consider the brawlings, fighting and altercations which are daily and hourly occuring on our streets, in our ale-houses, and saloons, together with thefts, robberies, and murders, and you have a faint picture of the condition of society to-day. To this dark list you may add "the haughtiness and oppression of those in authority—widows and orphans suffering injustice; fools, profligates, and tyrants rioting in wealth and abundance; generous actions unrewarded; crimes unpunished, and the vilest of men raised to stations of dignity and honor." Hence, we see on every hand discord, confusion, suffering, and strife marring the peace, harmony, and happiness of mankind. This is human society in every-day dress.

If there were nothing better in the universe for man, no realm where under better conditions he could develop the nobler elements of his nature, life would become a burden, and the future would lose its charm. To be born into a world of confusion, misery, and distress; to sail around for a while on life's rough and stormy sea, and then, on some dark and gloomy night to go down into everlasting confusion, or eternal nothingness, is not an inspiring or uplifting picture to contemplate. But we gladly turn away from human society to contemplate society as it is, and always will be, in that better country. We have family reunions on earth which often afford temporary pleasure, but they are far from being perfect. We do not, and cannot know what pleasure and delight are found in society when and where, everything is perfect. In contemplating the society in heaven several things are to be considered. First, we have pictured in the mind a country, or empire, the vastness and beauty of which is beyond all description. John had occasional glimpses of it, but they are only glimpses. What he saw and attempted to describe simply bewilders us. It is so far above anything that mortal eyes ever looked upon, that we can form but imperfect conceptions of its beauty and grandeur. There in that realm is the throne of God and the Lamb. There dwells the King in his beauty and glory, "in the eternal sunshine of whose countenance the host that worship at his feet will bask for-ever." Cherubim, seraphim, angels, and saints will compose the society of that better country. Doubtless some will be in advance of others in knowledge, but all will be perfectly happy and contented in their sphere; no prejudices nor jealousies will dwell in any soul. One family—all heirs of God, and joint (equal) heirs with Christ! Angels will be the familiar and constant companions of the saints. Does not the apostle, if not directly, indirectly refer to this when he says, "But ye are come unto Mount Sion, and unto the city of the living God, the heavenly Jerusalem, and to an innumerable company of angels, to the general assembly and church of the firstborn, which are written in heaven, and to God the Judge of all, and to the spirits of just men made perfect." We cannot realize what it will be to be immediately associated with angels. We somehow feel that they are above us, and in a sense that is true, but when we consider the interest they have taken in us, and the sympathy they have manifested toward us, we cannot but think that they will cause us to feel perfectly at home in their society. They know a great deal more about us now than we do about them. The Scriptures warrant us in the belief that the saints in their resurrection state are to be "equal unto the angels." What this implies and includes we may not know, but it means at least a fitness for each other's society. The angels will not be brought down to a level with the saints, but the saints will be lifted up to a level with the angels. The thought of being like Christ, made "equal unto the angels," and having them as familiar and loving companions is not only pleasing, but inspiring. This is no wild theory or speculation, but a fact—a blessed, glorious, scriptural fact. Poor old Lazarus, as we sometimes say, lying at the rich man's gate, desiring to be fed with crumbs, when the time came, was not compelled to wait until he got to heaven to be in company with the angels, for they came after him and carried him home. If the saints on earth could more fully realize the destiny that awaits them, they would not only think more about it, but quicken their steps toward it. Old Mr. Mead, when asked how he did, replied, "I am going home as fast as I can, as every honest man ought to do when his day's work is over; and I bless God that I have a good home to go to."

Another source of pleasure in that heavenly society will be that the saints of one age will associate and converse with saints of all other ages. Dr. Rolston says: "They shall hold converse with prophets and righteous men of olden times. They shall listen to the orations of Enoch and Elijah, of Abraham and Job, of Moses and Samuel, of David and Isaiah, of Daniel and Ezekiel, of Peter and James, of Paul and John. If a few moments on Mount Tabor, where Moses and Elijah talked with Jesus, so entranced the apostles, with what thrilling emotions must the souls of the redeemed be inspired when, on the eternal mount on high, they shall listen to the sublime orations in which so many eloquent and immortal tongues shall comment on the stupendous wonders of redemption!"

That will be no mean company, no ordinary society, composed of all the purest and best of earth and the highest and most noble of heaven. It is said that when Cyneas, the ambassador of Pyrrhas, returned from Rome he was asked what he thought of the city and state, and answered that it seemed to him to be a state of none but great statesmen, and a commonwealth of kings. "Such is heaven—no other than a parliament of emperors, a commonwealth of kings; every humble, faithful soul in that kingdom is coheir with Christ, hath a role of honor and a scepter of power, and a throne of majesty, and a crown of glory." But some humble Christian may say, "This is too much, more than can be expected, a thousand times more than I deserve." Very true, we deserve no such honor; but it comes as a gift—a free and unmerited gift. Come, my beloved, join with me; although a little in advance of time, we can repeat the words, if we miss the tune and utterly fail in the inspiration, "Unto him that loved us, and washed us from our sins in his own blood, and hath made us kings and priests unto God and his Father; to him be glory and dominion for ever and ever. Amen." *"Kings and Priests."*— Dr. Clark says the proper rendering is "a kingdom of priests, or a royal priesthood. The regal and sacerdotal dignitaries are the two highest that can possibly exist among men; and these two are here mentioned to show the glorious prerogatives and state of the children of God." This is no more than a faint description of the character of those who shall compose the society of heaven.

In that blissful realm love will reign supreme; like a chain of purest gold it will bind the inhabitants to each other and to the throne, for *God is love.* Paul knew something about the excellency and powers of love when he said, "Now abideth faith, hope, love, these three; and the greatest of these is love." Greatest on earth and greatest in heaven! Think of going out of a world full of hatred, malice, and revenge into a world where love reigns supreme—where it will shine out in every word, look, and act—and you have a picture of one of the elements of heavenly society.

"Love is the golden chain that binds
  The happy souls above;
And he's an heir of heaven who finds
  His bosom glow with love."

All the external splendor of the heavenly country would not make it a desirable place without a corresponding fitness for it. What would heaven be to a besotted libertine, to the one in whose heart wrangles hatred, enmity, malice, and revenge? "As a horse haltered by a golden chain to a marble manger filled with diamonds" would be miserable, so a corrupt, unwashed soul would be miserable in heaven.

Society in heaven will be on a much higher and broader plane than is to be found on earth. "It will not be a solitary niche for each individual to occupy. It will be the heavenly Jerusalem, the city of the living God, an innumerable company of angels, the spirits of just men made perfect, Jesus, the Mediator of all, and God, the judge of all. In that country the face will be a perfect and transparent exponent of the mind; the faintest word will be the truest embodiment of the thought. There will be no disturbing fears or perplexities without. All that corrupts and contaminates our social system will be excluded, and happy, because holy, men will be the inhabitants of that better country."

A more glowing description of the condition and state of the saints in heaven cannot be found than that given by John. It is not what he had read in books, nor what he had learned from others, but what he saw and heard for himself. "These are they which came out of great tribulation, and have washed their robes, and made them white in the blood of the Lamb. Therefore are they before the throne of God, and serve him day and night [without ceasing] in his temple: and he that sitteth on the throne shall dwell among them. They shall hunger no more, neither thirst any more; neither shall the sun light on them, nor any heat. For the Lamb which is in the midst of the throne shall feed them, and shall lead them unto living fountains of waters: and God shall wipe away all tears from their eyes." Is not the possibility, ah, the hope of being in that company inspiring and uplifting?

> "No wasting sorrow there is found,
>   No cheek is wet with burning tears;
> Whom those eternal walls surround
>   No foe can reach, no pang, no fear.
>
> Land of the blest, on faith's keen eye
>   Faint glimpses of thy glory break;
> Oh, when in earth's last sleep I lie,
>   'Mid thy full glory let me wake."

Heavenly Recognition.—Shall we know each other in heaven? This question in one form or another has been asked many, many times. Some have supposed that the change wrought in the resurrection will be of such a nature as to destroy all possible resemblance of the earthly body. That the change will be marvelous no one will care to question. The mortal shall put on immortality, the corruptible shall put on incorruption, the natural shall put on spiritual, and the weak shall put on strength. All this will occur in a moment, in the twinkling of an eye. Stupendous as the change may be, it will not destroy personal, conscious identity. Every saint as well as every sinner will be fully conscious that he is himself. If this be not so, then the doctrine of future rewards and punishments cannot be sustained. What meaning could we attach to Scriptures such as these? "For we must all appear before the judgment seat of Christ; that everyone may receive the things done in his body, according to that he hath done, whether it be good or bad." "Say ye to the righteous, that it shall be well with him: for they shall eat the fruit of their doings. Woe unto the wicked! it shall be ill with him: for the reward of his hands shall be given him." "Whatsoever a man soweth, that shall he also reap." "Knowing that of the Lord ye shall receive the reward of the inheritance: for ye serve the Lord Christ. But he that doeth wrong shall receive for the wrong he hath done: and there is no respect of persons." In the twenty-fifth chapter of Matthew our Lord teaches plainly and positively that the future eternal condition of man is contingent upon his doings in this life. This, of necessity, carries with it the doctrine of personal, conscious identity. Each will know himself, and that he possesses his own body. "I am the same identical person that lived on earth." This is implied in what Abraham said to the rich man, "Son, remember that thou in thy lifetime receivedst thy good things." Things of time will be remembered in eternity. This furnishes a strong presumptive proof of future recognition.

While the resurrection body will be entirely free from all infirmities and all imperfections, yet in form and appearance it will resemble the earthly body. There is no reason why it should not be so; it might as well resemble itself as somebody else. When our Lord appeared to his disciples after his resurrection, he appeared in his own body—the very body that hung on the cross. They saw him, handled him, and heard him speak. He is the first-fruit, and thereby teaches what the harvest shall be. He appeared in his own body, and in like manner the saints will appear, each in his own body. Dr. Goodwin says: "There will be a parting with flesh and blood, and all its deformities and deficiencies, ...but the glorified body will be cast in the mold of the earthly form. Identity of person, individuality of being, seem to require this."

While it is most reasonable to believe that the saints in heaven will know by sight those they have known on earth, the question arises as to how they will come to know those they never knew on earth. It may be by sight, or by a formal introduction, or by some instinct or intuition. In whatever manner it may be brought about, it will afford the most exquisite pleasure and delight. When I was a boy I was introduced to General Harrison and shook hands with him. That was a day of my life never to be forgotten. If it shall please the dear Master to receive me into his kingdom, I think it will afford me unspeakable pleasure and delight to know, and clasp the hand of Abraham, Moses, Elijah, and all the prophets and apostles. As I muse upon the possibilities of such an occurrence, a strange but delightful thrill goes through my very soul. When Moses and Elias appeared with Christ on Mount Tabor, the disciples knew them. But just how they came to know them, we are not informed. Moses had been dead fourteen hundred years, and Elijah was translated nine hundred years before this event; but there they were, and the disciples knew them. It is not unreasonable to believe that they knew them by a spiritual instinct, and so it may be with the saints in heaven. 'But considering the innumerable host—millions of millions,—how long will it take to form the acquaintance of all? No matter as to that; days, weeks, months, years, and centuries are not reckoned there. One word is all the calendar known in heaven. That word is ETERNITY!

> "To think, when heaven and earth are fled,
>   And times and seasons o'er,
> When all that can be shall be dead,
>   That I shall die no more;
> Oh, where will then my portion be?
> Were shall I spend eternity?"

Shall we know our loved ones in heaven somewhat as we know them here? It would seem most reasonable that we shall; only they will appear more lovely than they ever did upon earth. Perhaps the last time we saw them on earth they were old, infirm, crippled, or pale and emaciated; but now they are perfect, with the bloom of eternal youth stamped upon their cheek. We never saw a perfect human form; there are none such on earth. Sin has marred every countenance, dimmed every eye, and set its mark on every form, but the resurrection body will be perfect. While we shall know in heaven those whom we have known on earth and the relation we sustained to each other, it will not create a spirit of clannishness such as often obtains in human society; their presence will yield great pleasure and delight, and make heaven all the more sweet to us; but the heart attachment will be just as deep and abiding toward those we never knew on earth.

The religion of Jesus Christ, whether in heaven or upon earth, lifts its possessor above the spirit of mere clannishness. Did not our Lord teach some such doctrine while here on earth? On one occasion, while he was teaching in a certain house, his mother and brethren stood without and desired to speak to him. Some one informed him of their presence and desire. Then he said: "Who is my mother? and who are my brethren? ...Whosoever shall do the will of my Father which is in heaven, the same is my brother, and sister, and mother." Thus it will be in heaven— all bound to the throne of God and the Lamb and to each other by the cords of immortal love, and moving in the most perfect and delightful harmony. All family and ecclesiastical lines, such as are drawn on earth, will be forever excluded—one family, dwelling together in peace and joy. "They shall know as they are known."

Bishop N. Castle, D.D., says: "When this pilgrim path fades from sight; when the veil of flesh is rent asunder; when the heart-throb is no longer pulsed; when the tired limbs lie gently folded; when the dreamless sleep has stilled all, then immortal vision bursts upon the sight—'the King in his beauty,' 'the church of the first-born,' a numberless multitude, white-robed and triumphant, gathered from all time, all nations. Here Abraham and Lazarus, Moses and Elias, the martyrs and their companions, the pastor and his flock, the patriarch and the youthful, kindreds by flesh and in grace, meet in joyous recognition and celebration in the day-dawn that is eternal."

Rev. John Evans, the Welsh preacher, and his wife had lived together happily for many years. As old age came on they seemed to become more strongly attached to each other. One day, while Mrs. Evans was attending to her domestic affairs, and meditating on how it might be in the world to come, she suddenly stopped her work, and, standing in the doorway of Mr. Evans's study, said, "John, I have been thinking and wondering how it will be in heaven; do you really believe that we shall know each other there?" "Why, my dear," said he, "do you think we shall be bigger fools there than we are here? We know each other here, and shall we not know each other there? To be sure we shall."

Our thoughts are ever and anon invaded by questions concerning children in heaven. Shall we see them and know them there as we do here? "Will the mother, from whose arms her babe was taken, have it given back to her just as it was, an infant, when ten, twenty, or more years ago she kissed it for the last time?" Upon this question the Scriptures are silent, and we are left mainly to our own conjectures. My desire in this matter may be the basis of my faith; but, however that may be, I love to think of children in heaven as I see them on earth. They form an interesting part of human society, and so I think it will be in heaven. Cursed by sin as this world is, yet, what would it be without children? Children in heaven will not always remain children in knowledge. This is not necessarily implied in heavenly childhood. "A lily may be as perfect in its way as an oak, and the rose of Sharon as beautiful as the stately cedar of Lebanon."

If progress in heaven is gradual, and it certainly is, I see no good reason why the minds of children, when clothed with immortal bodies, might not be drawn out and developed without increasing the size of the immortal body.

Mental strength or intellectual culture is not contingent upon the size and form of the body here on earth; neither will it be in heaven. In a sense the saints will all be children in heaven; the wisest and best of them will not have learned the alphabet while on earth. Some of the smallest insects that float in the air around us are the most intelligent and beautiful. So it may be in heaven— children, all immortal and perfect, free from everything that would disturb or annoy; innocent and affectionate, basking in the light from the eternal throne; receiving the caresses of angels and smiles of recognition from the more advanced saints, until they are filled with rapture and delight— Oh, it seems to me that heaven will be all the richer if children are there!

We often think of loved ones who have gone from us, but we think of them in form somewhat as we saw and knew them here. We cannot think of them in some other form. Do parents think of their children whom God has taken to himself as adults in form and appearance? No, they cannot think of them thus; they think of them and expect to find them as they last saw them on earth. Many years ago God took two of mine to himself; I think of them in heaven as I saw them on earth. But if the saints are disappointed in this fond anticipation it will be a heavenly disappointment, and will be altogether satisfactory; each saint will say, "He hath done all things well."

There are innumerable theories and conjectures concerning the order of society, and recognition in that heavenly land. Some make it too ethereal, while others, doubtless, make it quite too material. It is difficult to settle on any well-defined idea between these two extremes. Some have society in heaven divided into groups, without any very direct communication with each other— a kind of distinction along social lines, not very different from earth-life. A little girl, who had just been dressed in a beautiful new gown, asked her mother . whether she would wear that dress in heaven. "No, my child." "How, then, will they know that I belong to the best society?" Dr. T. DeWitt Talmage says: "Christians in heaven will dwell in neighborhoods and clusters. I am sure that some people I shall like in heaven a great deal better than others." Some such thing may be true, but for the present I shall not incorporate it among my articles of faith.

The idea that I gather from the Holy Scriptures is that the inhabitants of heaven, saints and angels, compose one family, dwelling together in the most delightful harmony and bliss. While some may be in advance of others in knowledge, there will be no distinction along social lines. The saints will all sing the same song, worship before the same throne, and honor the same Redeemer. Every saint, from all the ages and from every clime, will fully realize that he is saved by grace, and that he owes it all to the Father, Son, and Holy Spirit.

> "Blest hour! when righteous souls shall meet—
>   Shall meet to part no more,
> And with celestial welcome greet
>   On an immortal shore;
>
> Each tender tie dissolved with pain
>   With endless bliss is crowned;
> All that was dead revives again,
>   All that was lost is found."

VIII
HEAVEN — HOME

HUMAN LIFE ON EARTH has been fitly represented as a pilgrimage, a journey, a voyage. The ancients were wont to speak of themselves as pilgrims, strangers, and sojourners. We are not, and cannot be stationary. Whether young or old, rich or poor, bond or free, we are moving. The earth turns upon its axis once in twenty-four hours, and makes its circuit around the sun once each year. Thus, in a whirl and in a curve, we are carried through space millions of miles every year. In like manner we are moving through time — fourteen hundred millions of persons, all moving at once, and in the same direction. None can stop if he would; on, on we go. "By an inexorable law we are all chained to the chariot-wheels of time. There is no bridling the steeds or leaping from the chariot; we must be constantly in motion." One every second, sixty every minute, three thousand six hundred every hour, eighty-six thousand four hundred every day, and thirty-one million five hundred and thirty-six thousand every year reach the end and pass into that "undiscovered country from whose bourn no traveler returns." Who, in contemplating such tremendous facts, can fail to realize that he is a sojourner, a wayfaring man?

This was the constant feeling of the patriarchs; they realized that here they had no continuing city, no certain abiding-place. As it was with the ancients, so it is with us; but the majority do not realize the fact. Thousands live as if they expected to stay here forever. That rich man of whom the Saviour spoke seemed not to realize that he was a sojourner. "I will pull down my barns, and build greater... And I will say to my soul, Soul, thou hast much goods laid up for *many years;* take thine ease, eat, drink, and be merry." Thus men act to-day. Seneca said, "It is the bounty of nature that we live, but of philosophy that we live well; which is, in truth, a greater benefit than life itself."

It is not so pleasing to think or speak of these things, but we must be true to ourselves; eternal consequences hinge upon them. Human life is a feeble and uncertain affair. It is beset on all sides with innumerable dangers. The marvel is, not that we die, but that we live. If it were "all of life to live," or "all of death to die," we might lash the steeds to greater speed; but, "there's the rub," for it is neither the one nor the other. There is life beyond and there is death beyond, and *as we sow, so shall we reap.* It is just; it ought to be so. "Shall not the Judge of all the earth do right?" A distinguished American divine said: "I think we ought to buoy ourselves in our course as we buoy a harbor. Off this shoal a black buoy floats, and says to those who sail by, as plainly as if it spoke in all languages, 'Keep to the right here'; and over against it floats another, and says, 'Keep to the left here.' Now, in life's ocean, wherever we know the quicksands are, wherever we have once been stranded, let us sink the buoy and anchor of memory and keep to the right or to the left, as the shoal may be."

The patriarchs desired a better country; they were looking for a city which had foundations, a habitation that would abide, a place they could call home. They were tired of tents and tabernacles, and longed for a house not made with hands—something permanent. Is that not the longing of every genuine Christian's heart? Whether he lives in a palace, cottage, or hovel, he knows that his stay is only temporary, that there is none abiding. Even though his house be preserved from the consuming flames and the fury of the storms, still he knows there is *none abiding*. Look up, my beloved, and be of good cheer, for the Lord has provided some better things for you. So he said to the patriarchs, and so he says to you.

When the hearts of the disciples were sad, Jesus said to them: "Let not your heart be troubled:… In my Father's house are many mansions." This scripture was referred to in a former chapter, but in this connection I wish to consider it under the idea of home. With but few exceptions, the most sacred place on earth is home. God intended that it should be so; for he "setteth the solitary in families." I do not speak simply of places where families live, but of home as God intended it should be. Such a home is the one place on earth where love, peace, and confidence reign supreme; where all "hearts are sure of each other." Such a home is on the mountaintops of cheerfulness, and is the center of joy, both "equatorial and tropical." The sailor on the high seas at the midnight hour, while the storm is raging, and the wounded soldier in the far-away hospital, think of home. The prodigal, though a besotted wreck, thought of home; so do wanderers now. To Adam, Paradise was home. To the good among his descendants, home is paradise. It is not so much the house, with its plain furniture, nor the "old oaken bucket that hung in the well," that draws so heavily upon the heart, but the associations—father, mother, brother, sister. But for these, home would not be half so sacred in memory's storehouse. The thoughts of home often cheer the heart in the midst of the cares, toils, and anxieties of life. "'I am going home,' thinks the shopman when he bars his heavy doors and closes his windows at night, tired with the labors of the day. 'I must hurry home,' says the mother whose heart is on her babe in the cradle. 'Oh, how I long to get home,' says the schoolboy, disconsolate over the hopeless task. 'Don't stop me; I am going home,' says the bright-eyed girl, skipping along the foot-path. 'I am almost home,' says the dying Christian, 'and then no more sorrow nor sighing forever; almost home.'"

What beautiful and tender associations cluster around that word *home*. A few there may be whose hearts are too deeply depraved to care for home, but I do not envy their feelings. Fifty years had come and gone when I visited the old homestead. Everything, except the ground, appeared to be changed; but memory, true to her trust, called back the days and years long since gone. As I stood on the spot where the old house stood there passed before my vision, like a panorama, the happy group of a dozen persons gathered around the hearth of that old-fashioned fire-place. Unbidden tears dimmed my eyes as the question came, "Where are they? Eight have gone beyond, only four remain." (Only two now.) Will we never meet again as in the long ago? Never, no never! Oh, if this were all, the very thought of home, and home associations on earth, however tender, would be painful; and I should prefer a charge of cruelty against memory for holding fast to scenes and associations that well-nigh crush the heart. But it is not all. Somewhere in the vast universe there is a home for the soul. Our own consciousness says so, reason says so, and God says so. A brother, in taking leave of an afflicted sister, said, "I shall probably not see you again in the land of the living." She replied, "Brother, I trust we shall meet in the land of the living; we are now in the land of the dying."

Our Lord very well understood the tender feelings of the human heart concerning earthly homes. He had told his disciples that he was going away; that he could not remain with them visibly. This troubled and perplexed them. Then he said: "In my Father's house are many mansions: ...I go to prepare a place for you." "Father's house"—this would very naturally suggest the idea of home and home associations. He would not have them think of heaven as a strange country inhabited by strangers. No; it is Father's house; it is home, I am going to Father's house—my Father and your Father. Then "I will come again, and receive you unto myself; that where I am, there ye may be also." An old divine said: "When I was a boy I thought of heaven as a great, shining city, with vast walls, and domes, and spires, and with no body in it except white, tenuous angels, who were strangers to me. By and by my little brother died, and I thought of a great city with walls, and domes, and spires, and a flock of cold, unknown angels, and one little fellow I was acquainted with. He was the only one I knew at that time. Then another brother died; and there were two that I knew. Then my acquaintances began to die, and the flock continually grew. But it was not till I had sent one of my little children to his grandparent—God—that I began to think I had got a little in myself. A second went; a third went; a fourth went; and by that time I had so many acquaintances in heaven that I did not see any more walls, and domes, and spires. I began to think of the residents of the celestial city. And now so many of my acquaintances have gone there that it sometimes seems to me that I know more in heaven than I do on earth."

Beloved, what are your thoughts of heaven? Does it appear to you as a great city—a far-away country filled with strangers? Do you think of the angels as altogether strangers to you, treating you as strangers often treat each other in this world? Do you think of the inhabitants being divided into groups, and forming a thousand and one circles in society? Do you think of upper and lower grades in society? Dismiss all such cold thoughts from your mind, and think of heaven as "Father's house" — my Father's house, where one child is just as near and dear as another. Away with all thoughts of partiality! *All saved by grace,* all clothed with robes, washed and made white in the blood of the Lamb! That will be home — the only place in the universe where the soul will feel perfectly at home. And as for the angels, they know a great deal more about you than you do about them. Don't you know that they are in sympathy with you all the time? Don't you know that they are "all ministering spirits, sent forth to minister for them who shall be heirs of salvation"? Don't you know that they encamp round about them that fear the Lord? Don't you know that they have been on the wing between heaven and earth ever since man was created? Don't you know that they are sent as escorts to accompany the saints home? Did they not come like a bright cloud to escort the divine Redeemer to the throne? Did they not come to the very gate of the rich man to carry Lazarus home? Don't you know that when the time for the great home-gathering is come the Son of man will "send his angels with a great sound of a trumpet, and they shall gather together his elect from the four winds, from one end of heaven to the other"? Do you think that after all this interest in you and sympathy for you, after the home-gathering is all over and past, they will flock off in a company by themselves as little too high to associate with you? No, my beloved, that will not be the order in heaven. The angels will be your familiar companions, for our Lord said concerning the saints that they "neither marry, nor are given in marriage: ...for they are equal unto angels."

When the home-gathering is all complete and the last saint is within the jasper walls, there will be a reunion worthy the name, such as was never witnessed by men or angels — the saints, all clothed upon with immortality, but tangible bodies, fashioned like unto the glorified body of

Heaven's Escort *(page 129)*

"For the Lord himself shall descend from heaven with a shout, with the voice of the archangel, and with the trump of God: and the dead in Christ shall rise first: then we which are alive and remain shall be caught up together with them in the clouds, to meet the Lord in the air: and so shall we ever be with the Lord" (I Thess. 4:16, 17)

Jesus Christ; the angels, with visible forms, all clothed in robes of spotless white, millions of millions, all gathered in the central empire of the universe; a soft, mellow, but brilliant light emanating from the throne of God and the Lamb, falling equally and alike on every part of the great city; the mists all cleared away; and without a shadow anywhere; all eyes turned upon the divine Redeemer, for it will be through him and by him that the glory of the eternal Father will be manifest—then, for the first time (for they have never all been together before), in one grand chorus they will sing: "Unto him that loved us, and washed us from our sins in his own blood, and hath made us kings and priests unto God and his Father; to him be glory and dominion for ever and ever. Amen." Is not the possibility, the reasonable and strong hope of being numbered with an innumerable company enough to inspire within us a fiery zeal to go through thick and thin to reach it? Paul caught a glimpse of it, and in his epistles it is recorded that he pressed for it, wrestled for it, ran for it, and fought for it, and when the home-gathering comes he will be there. O my soul! "What will it be to be there?"

> "O land of love! O land of light divine!
> Father, all-wise, eternal!
> Guide me, oh, guide these wandering feet of mine
> Into those gates supernal."

Dr. G. M. Mathews says: "Of all the descriptions of heaven none touch me so deeply as that familiar image which Jesus employed in the fourteenth chapter of John to portray it as a home. 'In my Father's house!' How warm and tender and restful that thought is to the pilgrim Christian. Heaven is the antitype of our tent home. Our faith has bright visions of the heavenly home where broken fellowships are renewed, family ties reknit, long separated friends recognized, disappointments, mistakes, and heartburnings unknown, and where in the progressiveness of the immortal life new discoveries are made and deep mysteries are revealed. The consciousness of being at such a home at last where these joyous conditions are abiding and eternal is the sweetest thought of heaven. The assurance that this better home will never be dissolved or disturbed is enough to fill the soul with rapturous delight. Glorious home, radiant with light and love!"

Concerning the etiquette in heaven we have no certain information, but we have a right to suppose that it will be of a very high order. It will not be stiff and arbitrary as it is often found in human society. It will be home etiquette, such as properly belongs to a family where love, peace, confidence, and harmony reign supreme. The angels are intelligent beings, and the saints when all immortal and glorified will be intelligent. "They shall know as they are known." In such a family of pure, sinless, intelligent beings we have a right to expect the most beautiful and enjoyable order. There will be no partiality, no evil surroundings, no jealousies, but confidence, utmost confidence in each other. The countenance of each will be the true index of all that is within. Every word, every act, and every look will be peaceful and loving, all heirs of God, joint heirs with Christ, and "equal unto the angels."

As heretofore intimated, we do not know just how the different members of this vast family will become acquainted with each other. Whether by formal introduction or by a divine intuition, we cannot tell; but, however that may be, it will be attended with the most exquisite pleasure and delight. If eternity were measured by years or ages, we might suppose that it would require many ages to become acquainted with each other. But years and ages are not reckoned there. If it should take millions of years, as we reckon time, there would always be an eternity before us, so that it will make no possible difference whether the acquaintance comes by intuition and at once, or during the eternal ages. There are elements in human society which will survive in heaven, only in a much higher and purer sense. Love, peace, joy, kindness, confidence, and sympathy will never die. In our thoughts of heavenly society we are not to make it too common nor too uncommon. Each saint will be himself—fully conscious that he is himself. There are powers which inhere in the soul that will never die. These, under more favorable conditions, such as heaven will afford, will shine out in clearer light than was possible while on earth.

In our contemplations of that better country two things should be kept in mind: (1) *The vastness of that empire.*—The sun, which is the center of our solar system, is more than one million two hundred thousand times larger than the earth. In other words, it would take one million two hundred thousand worlds the size of the earth to make one equal to the sun. Now, it is not unreasonable to believe that the heaven of heavens, the place of the eternal throne, the central empire of the universe, is many times larger than the sun. (2) *The number of the inhabitants.*—It is estimated that fourteen hundred millions of persons live upon the earth at one time, and this vast number passes away every thirty-three years. Now, suppose that ten hundred millions of these enter heaven; then you count back generation after generation, and forward generations yet to come, and who can estimate the number of the inhabitants? When John saw the company he said it was "a great multitude, which no man could number." Then add to this the host of angels. Paul calls it an "innumerable company," and John says, "The number of them was ten thousand times ten thousand, and thousands of thousands." Chiliads of chiliads, and myriads of myriads; that is, an infinite or innumerable multitude.

This calculation does not rest upon mere conjecture, for underneath it is a Scripture basis, especially in that which relates to the number of the inhabitants. The saints and angels will not dwell *in* each other like compressed air, but *with* each other. Each will have a separate, personal existence. Each will have form, shape, visibility, and tangibility, and hence of necessity will occupy some space. Now, take the number of inhabitants to be as John represents it, and no small country like this earth would accommodate them. Thus, reasoning from such data as we have, the conclusion is that heaven is a vast empire, surpassing in magnitude, grandeur, and beauty any other world in the universe. We are too much inclined to weigh and measure heavenly things by earthly things, half forgetting that the things seen are temporal, while the things unseen are spiritual and eternal. Dr. Hamilton, in speaking of this family—all at home—says: "What a heavenful of princely creatures the eternal Father will have when all the redeemed are presented to him in the brightness of his Son's glory, even as the Son is the brightness of his glory. Christ has said that they shall shine like so many suns in the kingdom of the Father,—a whole heavenful of glorious-bodied creatures, each one emitting a splendor like the glorious body of the Lord. 'Now are we the sons of God, and *it doth not yet appear what we shall be:* but we know that, when he shall appear, we shall be like him; for we shall see him as he is.'" This is but a dim and imperfect description of heaven as a home. Who can anticipate the delightful home feeling that will come over the soul when Father's house of many mansions is reached? Now, amid the storms and conditions of life, the pilgrim stranger often looks homeward and hopes that by and by he will reach it. The fact of being at home is one thing, and the home feeling is quite another and different thing. We have places on earth which we call home, and to us, in many respects, they are desirable and pleasant. But to make them complete three things are always lacking. These are safety, permanency, and completeness. Whether it be a palace, cottage, or hovel, there is always a feeling of insecurity. Flames may consume, thieves and robbers may invade, and sickness and death may come in at any moment. Then we know to an absolute certainty that it is not permanent; that it is only a temporary stopping-place. Either it will be taken from us, or we will be taken from it; "there is none abiding." However fine and richly furnished our earthly homes may be, they are not quite up to our ideal of perfection. There is always something lacking. We change here and there, and add this and that, but still it is not faultless. Not so in Father's house of many mansions. That home once entered, there will come to the soul the delightful consciousness of safety, permanency, and completeness. Whatever more our Saviour intended to teach by Father's house of "many mansions," it is perfectly safe to infer that he intended us to understand that the place, with all the arrangements and provisions, was ample and complete. That home once entered, the soul, for the first time in the history of its existence, will be able to say, as never before, SATISFIED.

While on the pilgrimage, with heaven in view—

> "The soul for joy *unfolds* her wings
> And loud her lovely sonnet sings,
>   'I'm going home.'"

The pilgrimage ended—

> "The soul for joy *fold* her wings
> And loud her lovely sonnet sing,
>   'I'm safe at home.'"

How far is it home? This question in one form or another is often suggested to the mind, and we cannot help it; and unless we become over-anxious about it, there is nothing sinful in the thought. If we are going to that better country we will naturally think a great deal about it—its dimensions, location, and distance. Concerning the distance and location we have nothing definite to guide us, but the prevailing opinion is that it is far away from the earth. From the intimations gathered from the sacred writers this opinion is well founded. Thoughts upon this subject may be helpful in so far as they may tend to broaden our views of the magnitude and grandeur of the marvelous works of God. Paul was "caught up to the third heaven." Three heavens are spoken of in the Scriptures: First, the atmosphere—firmament. Second, the starry heavens—sun, moon, planets, and stars. Third, the heaven of heavens, or the throne of the divine glory. The third, then, is above the starry heavens.

Now, let us consider this for one moment. The sun, in round numbers, is ninety-three millions of miles from our globe; but this mighty distance is but a step as compared with the distance to the stars, which appear to us as only little points of light in the distant heavens. Light, the swiftest force in nature, moves at the rate of one hundred and eighty-six thousand miles in a second of time. The nearest fixed stars are concluded by astronomers to be twenty trillions of miles from the earth. Swift as the motion of light is, it would take it three years to reach our globe. A cannon-ball, moving at the rate of five hundred miles an hour, would not reach those stars in less than four million five hundred thousand years. Professor Bessel, speaking of the star 61 Cygni, says it is distant from our globe more than sixty-two trillions of miles, and light, swift as it is, would require more than ten years to reach the earth. A cannonball, moving five hundred miles an hour, would require more than fourteen millions of years to go from our globe to Cygni. From these fairly well-established facts it would appear that the stars are luminous bodies of immense size, and shine by their own native light, and are centers of worlds and systems, as our sun is the center of the worlds around it. I have mentioned these few facts to show the magnitude of the universe, and, also, that heaven is a great way off. Paul was caught up to the third heaven, which must have been above the first and second heavens. Held to this little planet by some invisible force, with occasional glimpses of distant worlds, we are left to wonder what there may be in the boundless realm of space, the center of which is everywhere, and boundary nowhere.

If then, heaven is so far away, how long will it take a soul to reach it after it is freed from the body? That is a question for the angels to answer, and not for me. They have been coming and going back and forth ever since the morning of time, so that they know all about it. No one can tell how swiftly a spirit or spiritual body can pass through the air. It may outstrip the velocity of light a thousandfold. Who can form any conception of the velocity of thought? Light, swiftly as it moves, would be too slow a coach to travel with thought. Judging from the frequent visitations of the angels, the appearance of Moses and Elias with Christ on the mount, and what our Lord said to the thief on the cross, the intervening space between heaven and earth will be passed through very quickly.

The Scriptures continually hold forth the idea that heaven is above, and far away. "A glorious high throne from the beginning is the place of our sanctuary:" "Heaven is my throne, and the earth is my footstool"—heaven, a universe in itself, around which, on all sides, move in silent grandeur, worlds, and systems of worlds, all in full view of the immortal vision of the saints. And as they behold this magnificent display of the wisdom, power, and benevolence of God they will simultaneously exclaim, "Great and marvellous are thy works, Lord God Almighty; just and true are thy ways, thou King of saints." This, my beloved, is Father's house of many mansions; this is home, with all that home means in the highest and purest sense.

Heaven is represented as being above: Christ was "carried *up into* heaven"; "I saw the Lord sitting upon a throne, *high* and lifted up"; far "as the heaven is high above the earth"; "when he ascended *up* on *high,*" "far above all heavens." Not only above all heavens, but *far* above them. The pious and devoted Bishop Pearson says: "Whatever heaven there is above all the rest which are called heavens; whatever sanctuary is holier than all which are called holies; whatsoever place is of greatest dignity in all of these courts above, into that place did the Lord ascend where in the splendor of his deity he was before he took upon himself our humanity. We learn from this, then, for certain, that in none of the planets or stars, visible or invisible, in what is called the second heaven, is to be sought the final abode of the blest, but it is far beyond them."

I shall close this chapter with a quotation from Dr. E. Adkins: "The saints will be blessed with a delightful sense of home—home, the dearest spot on earth, the scene of our purest enjoyments. But oh, how precious are all its pleasures and endearments in such a world as this! How few, comparatively, are favored with a genuine home. The greater part of mankind are wanderers, sojourners, tenants at will. And this is the lot of God's dear children as well as others. But even at best an earthly home fails to satisfy the innate longings of the soul. The Creator has placed within us aspirations which conform to a nobler, happier destiny. Those who are made heirs of God according to the hopes of eternal salvation are sensible of this, and cheerfully acquiesce in the thought that they have here no certain dwelling-place, nor perfect objects of affection, while they look upward with joyful anticipations to their future heavenly home. And these hopes will not be disappointed when Christ shall take his elect to himself, when they shall receive their inheritance in his everlasting kingdom, and dwell in the blest mansions prepared for them. Kings' palaces are but temporary, comfortless booths compared with the everlasting habitation into which they will be received; and the sweetest domestic enjoyments are scarcely a foretaste of the blessedness of those heavenly connections and associations amid which they will dwell. There will be no precariousness, no imperfection attendant upon that blissful home. In it the feeble earthly foretaste will be exchanged for complete fruitions; the soul's indefinite longing will be satisfied, its ideal realized. Home with God, with loved ones, among kindred spirits, loving and beloved, and in the midst of all things lovely—what more could be desired?"

"That great, mysterious Deity
We soon with open face shall see;
   The beatific sight
Shall fill the heavenly courts with praise,
And wide diffuse the golden blaze
   Of everlasting light."

IX
HEAVEN — REST

"Beyond life's toils and cares,
Its hopes and joys, its weariness and sorrow,
Its sleepless nights, its days of smiles and tears,
Will be a long sweet life unnumbered by years,
One bright unending morrow.

"No aching hearts are there,
No tear-dimmed eyes, no form by sickness wasted,
No cheek grown pale through penury or care,
No spirits crushed beneath the woes they bear,
No sighs for bliss untasted."

LONG AGO SOME ONE said, "I am weary of my life." A little later another said, "Oh, that I had wings like a dove! for then would I fly away, and be at rest." Still later, a voice came ringing down from the skies, "Arise ye, and depart; for this is not your rest." Finally, another said, "There remaineth therefore a rest to the people of God." Life on earth is full of care, toil, and weariness. It must needs be so. When man sinned God said unto him, "In the sweat of thy face shalt thou eat bread." Thus has it been through all the ages. There is physical, mental, and moral work to perform, all of which produces more or less weariness to the physical man. Solomon says, "Much study is a weariness of the flesh." Labor of any sort is a tax upon the flesh. The mind does not weary, but the brain through which it operates grows weary. To cultivate the ground, develop the intellect, and use the moral powers properly is laborious. But man is made for activity, even though it produces weariness. Idleness is not only hurtful, but sinful as well. This is not the time, nor earth the place, for permanent rest. "The law of nature," says Dr. Ruskin, "is, that a certain quantity of work is necessary to produce a certain quantity of good of any kind whatever. If you want knowledge you must toil for it; if food, you must toil for it; and if pleasure, you must toil for it."

Everything in nature moves. From the particle of dust at our feet, to a man, all bear the impress of the law of labor. Action is man's salvation physically, mentally, and morally. "He only is truly wise who lays out to work till life's latest hour, and that is the man who will live the longest and live to the best purpose." Idleness and worry kill more persons than work. Activity with cheerfulness is healthful; yet, all labor on earth is attended with more or less weariness, and the physical man will wear out.

But it is not labor in a general way of which I wish to speak particularly, but of Christian work or labor in the Church of Christ. In this vast field there is something for everyone to do. As in nature, so in grace. The law of action in the kingdom of grace is just as binding and universal as in the realm of nature. Show me an idler in the visible Church of Christ and I will show you a dwarf in Christian experience. Our Lord, both by precept and example, taught the law of labor in the kingdom of grace. "I must work the works of him that sent me while it is day: the night cometh when no man can work." Peter, who knew all about Christ's manner of life while on earth, said he "went about doing good." He did good to the souls and bodies of men. His was a busy life. From morning till evening, and oftentimes in the night season he was at work. If one so pure and faultless as he felt the necessity and importance of toiling, how should his disciples feel? He was often weary. John says, "Jesus being wearied... sat thus on the well." So Christians often grow weary in the work, but should never grow weary of the work. "Let us not be weary in well doing: for in due season we shall reap, if we faint not." Neander, as he closed his eyes in death said, "I am weary; I will go to sleep. Good-night."

Jesus said to the idlers, "Go work to-day in my vineyard." That commandment is in full force to-day. The apostles, having learned from both the precepts and the example of the Master, were all busy men. They toiled day and night to build up and extend the kingdom of Christ. James struck the key-note when he said, "Shew me thy faith without thy works, and I will shew thee my faith by my works." This appears to have been one article in the apostolic creed. What a heroic worker Paul was; here and there, day and night, always at it—running, wrestling, pressing, and fighting, not always in sunshine, but often in sorrow and weariness. Let him speak for himself: "Of the Jews five times received I forty stripes save one. Thrice was I beaten with rods, once was I stoned, thrice I suffered shipwreck, a night and a day I have been in the deep; in journeyings often, in perils of waters, in perils of robbers, in perils by mine own countrymen, in perils by the heathen, in perils in the city, in perils in the wilderness, in the sea, in perils among false brethren; in weariness and painfulness, in watchings often, in hunger and thirst, in fastings often, in cold and nakedness." Yet he said, "None of these things move me." Other of the apostles fared no better than he, but they toiled on, and to-day they know what it is to rest.

The crying need of the world to-day is for more Christian workers—heroic, consecrated workers. More than half the people have not yet heard the gospel of salvation. This is not the time nor the place for rest. The evening draws on apace; what is to be done must be done quickly. The night cometh when no man can work. Souls are perishing all around us. "Some one is sinking to-day." "Say not that it is yet four months and then cometh the harvest." It is here now, the field is white; reap to-day, for to-morrow you may not be here. There is work for the head, heart, hands, and feet. The Master of the vineyard sees you, and angels are looking upon you. See! The sick are to be visited, the hungry fed, the naked clothed, the sorrowful comforted, the cast-down lifted up, and the tempted encouraged. Oh! The world is brimful of work, and the time is short.

While some men attach too much importance to work, others attach too little to it. Faith and works are not only friends, but familiar companions. In building up Christian character neither can go without the other. Dr. Cowdray says, "As in a building, after the foundation is laid, great labor, diligence, and expense is necessary to finish and furnish it, even so in the heavenly edifice of the soul." All our lifetime is to be employed in the building of the walls and other parts of our spiritual structure, by the exercise of all virtues and by diligent observance of all of God's commandments, without which it will be as useless to look for salvation as it would be to expect to have a house simply because a foundation had been laid. Read Matt. 25:31-47 and learn therefrom what Christ says about good works. Good works alone will not save a soul; neither will faith alone. They go together in building up Christian character, and are made a condition of entering into that everlasting rest. Rest to an idler means very much less than it does to one who is accustomed to toil. The Spirit, through John, said: "Blessed are the dead which die in the Lord from henceforth: ...they may rest from their labours." To one like Paul or John such an utterance of the Spirit is full of meaning; but what meaning would an idler attach to it? A bishop in the Episcopal Church says, "When I was about entering the ministry, I was one day in conversation with an old Christian friend, who said, 'You are to be ordained; when you are ordained, preach to sinners as you find them; tell them to believe in the Lord Jesus Christ, and they shall be just as safe as if they were in heaven; and then tell them to *work like horses.*"

We should not be too anxious to find rest on earth. Too many retire from active service long before they should. "Rest is for heaven, toil for earth." He that would enjoy rest must first toil. Everything on earth is transient. "Here have we no continuing city," no permanent resting-place.

"In the midst of life we are in death." It is said that an Indian chief, with his tribe, fled across a broad river to escape from the devouring flames of a prairie fire. When they were all safe across the river, he stuck his tent-pole in the ground and exclaimed, "Alabama!"—here we rest. But was it so? No; for they were soon visited and destroyed by a hostile tribe. So we seek in vain to find rest among the dying and the dead. *Earth has no Alabama.*

But there is rest in heaven. We should not, however, fall into the mistake of supposing that rest in that better country means a state of inactivity; some are wont to believe that when the saints enter heaven they will quietly sit down and in a kind of half-conscious manner while away the unnumbered ages of eternity. No; there will be something in heaven to do. The mind, unless radically changed, cannot rest in a state of inactivity. While this thought was considered in another chapter, we think it not improper to mention it in this connection. Progress is the law of the mind. Life on earth is too short to unfold all the powers of the mind. Man, at his best in this world, is only a beginner. The wisest and most learned realize this. It would be a reflection on the wisdom and benevolence of the Creator to allow that he endowed man with mental and moral powers to lie dormant throughout all the ages of eternity. God never did an unwise or unnecessary thing. President Mahan, D.D., says: "The most sublime feature in the human mind is its law of unlimited progress. Place it under circumstances favorable for development, and there is no limit to its onward progress. Verily, such minds were made for heaven, made for a sphere where God is to be known, where we come into perfect sympathy with the Infinite Mind, and where both mental and moral powers will be eternally active, and where, consequently, such attainments as angels possess will be our perfect blessedness." Man, as he now is, with every avenue through which the mind operates crippled and imperfect, must advance but slowly. But, make all the avenues perfect, as they will be in heaven, and who can conceive of that to which the human mind will attain?

In the resurrection the mind will have a body suited to its own nature. The mortal shall put on immortality, the corruptible shall put on incorruption, the natural shall put on spiritual, and the weak shall become strong. In this resurrection body every avenue through which the mind communicates with outer things will be perfect—the brain clear as ether, the vision brighter than the sun at noon-day, and the consciousness all aglow with sensibility; to what may we not expect the mind to attain in such a condition? Because of the weak and crippled conditions of our mortal bodies the soul is hampered; it can only see in part, and understand in part. The eyes tire in seeing in a glass darkly; the brain wearies in supporting the mind in its search after knowledge; the head aches, and the nerves become unstrung, and we are compelled to stop and wait for recuperation. But in heaven it will not be thus. Much study will be rest, and the eye will never become tired in viewing terrestrial and celestial things.

Keeping in mind the thought that the saints in heaven will be in a condition to advance a thousandfold more rapidly than while on earth, we are not to overlook the fact that ample provisions have been made for the most active operations of the mind. "It is not probable that launched abroad upon such a universe there will be any lack of created things, the study of which will forever reveal more of God; nor will there be any lack of intelligent beings with whom we may have the sweet intercourse of mind with mind, and heart with heart." Within the range of the immortal vision, worlds and systems of worlds will appear, which are now far beyond the reach of the astronomer. Stars which appear to us as little points of light in the faraway heavens will be seen as vast worlds, millions of times larger than the earth. The history of all these worlds will be studied. For aught we know, angels will be our instructors. Since the angels have visited this little world so often, since they escort disembodied spirits to heaven, and since Moses and Elias came to talk with Christ on the mount, it is not unreasonable to believe that the saints, accompanied by angels, will, during the eternal ages, visit and revisit worlds and systems of worlds. Whether or not any of those worlds are inhabited, we cannot tell, but it is no sin to believe that they are. By and by "we shall see as we are seen, and know as we are known." There, in that Fatherland, we shall find our "Alabama." Hallelujah! Amen.

Bishop R. S. Foster, in speaking of the employment and progress of the saints in light, says: "To my mind, when I look in the direction of the future, one picture always arises—a picture of ravishing beauty. Its essence I believe to be true. It is that of a soul forever growing in knowledge, love, and in holy endeavor; that of a vast community of spirits, moving along a pathway of light of ever-expanding excellence and glory; heightening as they ascend; becoming more and more like the unpicturable pattern of Infinite Perfection; loving with an ever-deepening love; glowing with an ever-increasing fervor; rejoicing in ever-advancing knowledge; growing in power and glory. They are all immortal. There are no failures or reverses in any of them. Ages fly away; they soar on with tireless ages, and cycles advance toward them and retire behind them; still they soar, and shout, and unfold."

But aside from the beauty and grandeur of the place with its surrounding scenery; aside from the delightful associations; aside from the ever-increasing visions of glory, there will be rest—rest in the full meaning of that word. While we may not know how to connect continual activity with rest, yet so it will be in heaven. No one will be heard to say, "I am weary of my life." No one will say, "Oh that I had wings like a dove! for then would I fly away, and be at rest."

There will be the rest of complete contentment and satisfaction. These are blessings not known on earth. We may have had moments of contentment and satisfaction, but they were transient. They come and go like a rift in the clouds, which is quickly followed by a shadow. The patriarchs could not find such a place. They looked for it, but could not find it. Then they turned their thoughts toward a better country, a city of foundations. The rich on earth, who have everything within easy reach, are no more content and no better satisfied than are the poor. They all want something different, something better. Wished-for changes are made, but it does not bring complete satisfaction. A poor man with a large family, whose neighbor, without children, had suddenly become rich, peevishly complained that "God sent riches to others and children to him." Then, the scale turned in the poor man's favor and he became rich. But one by one his children were taken from him, and when he buried his last daughter he remembered with a sad heart his former murmurings and discontent. This is a picture of human life. In one way or another discontentment and dissatisfaction are everywhere. But in heaven it is not thus. Every aspiration and desire of the soul has been foreseen and provided for. Contentment and satisfaction will appear in every countenance.

There will be perfect rest from all fear and anxiety, such as often disturb here. The least of men know something about it. Paul speaks of fightings without and fear within. A thousand dangers beset us and our loved ones all the time; so that there are times when fear and anxiety almost unfit us for the duties of life. It will be widely different in heaven—no fear of present harm or future distress. There will come to the saints the ever-blessed and soul-satisfying consciousness of perfect safety—nothing to hurt or destroy in all the habitation of the saints.

"Out of the shadow of sadness,
Into the sunshine of gladness,
Into the light of the blessed;
Out of a land very dreary,
Out of the world of the weary,
Into the rapture of rest."

The saints in heaven will rest from temptation. There is no source of evil against which the Christian should be more guarded and better fortified than this one. Temptations are both negative and positive, direct and indirect. Christians are as often tempted not to do right things as they are to do wrong things. Satan, the arch-tempter, is a wily foe. He comes in a thousand ways, through agents and instrumentalities; not always, nor generally, in his real character, but as an angel of light. The Scriptures abound with counsel and instruction concerning this foe of God and man. He and his legions are arrayed against the church of Christ and everything that is good and pure. He is bent on the wreck and ruin of as many souls as possible. With what malice and hellish hatred he assaulted the Son of God. Forty days and nights the contest raged in the wilderness. From that day until now he has been in hot pursuit of the followers of Christ. Many who started well for the kingdom have been led out of the way. Turning to the Scriptures, we read: "Your adversary the devil, as a roaring lion, walketh about, seeking whom he may devour." "Put on the whole armour of God, that ye may be able to stand against the wiles of the devil." "Ye are in heaviness through manifold temptations." This is the lot of all Christians while on earth. Dr. Payson said: "Oh, the temptations which have harassed me for the last three months! I have met with nothing like them in books. It seems to me that my state has been far worse than that of Mansoul (Bunyan) when Diabolus and his legion broke into the town. They could not get into the castle—the heart; but my castle is full of them."

But, severe as the temptations are, they may be overcome. We cannot prevent them from coming, but, by the promised aid, we can resist and overcome them. When the Declaration of Independence was signed, Patrick Henry said, "Eternal vigilance is the price of liberty." So in the moral contest, "eternal vigilance" is the price of eternal salvation. Dr. Guthrie says, "Who sleeps by a magazine of gunpowder needs to take care even of sparks." Jesus said to his disciples, and to us as well, "What I say unto you I say unto all, Watch." But look up, tired, tempted one, relief is coming. The contest will not last forever. The country to which you are going is far above and beyond the range of the tempter's power. How sweet it will be to rest with the blessed consciousness that temptation will never enter that realm!

The saints will rest from labor. So the Spirit said to John, "They may rest from their labours; and their works do follow them." Spurgeon said to his people, many of whom were laborers, "O weary sons and daughters of Adam, you will not have to drive the plowshare into the unthankful soil in heaven; you need not to rise to daily toils before the sun hath risen, and labor till the sun hath long gone to his rest; but ye shall be still, ye shall be quiet, ye shall rest. Toil, trouble, and labor are words that cannot be spelled in heaven. They have no such thing there, for they always rest."

But I shall not attempt to name everything from which the saints in heaven will rest. Each heart knows its own sorrow. No two experiences are exactly alike. But whatever troubles and perplexes, whatever worries and annoys, whatever gives pain in the body or mind, whatever grieves and distresses—from all these the saints will rest; not temporarily, but forever and ever. "Heaven! oh, heaven! who does not desire to know all that may be known of it? Heaven! it is our Father's house, the home of angels and of all departed saints who have fallen asleep in Jesus. Heaven! it is the home of all our hopes; the end of life's weary pilgrimage, where we all at last expect to dismiss our burdens, to forget our sorrows, and to wipe away our tears."

It is no dream, no wild speculation, no delusion; there is a better country far above and away from this little sin-polluted earth, to which we are held by some invisible force. God has provided some better things for those that love him. Be of good cheer; you shall rest by and by. Poor you may be in this world,—you may not own a foot of land nor a cottage in this wilderness,—but listen to one of the most sublime and inspiring truths that ever fell on mortal ears, "Heirs of God, and joint-heirs with Christ." What does all this mean? It means more than earth, more than heaven, more than all worlds combined. It means God, who is greater, infinitely greater, than all created things. God created the soul and endowed it with such powers that nothing less than himself can be a satisfying portion. "Joint-heirs with Jesus Christ"—to share with him in the eternal glory of the Father; to share with him in all that heaven is, and all that heaven means. This, weary, tired, sorrowful one, is the destiny that awaits you. With such a prospect before you, made sure by the promise of God, can't you hold out a little longer? It will soon be here. Oh, that blessed to-morrow! Heaven, home, rest!

> "Dread not the valley thou mayest pass;
>   Fear not, the conflict soon is o'er;
> Trust Him; he's faithful to the last,
>   He'll lead thee to the happy shore;
> And thou shalt find, oh, welcome sight!
> At evening time it shall be light."

X
HEAVEN — SOURCES OF HAPPINESS

"There is a land where everlasting suns
Shed everlasting brightness; where the soul
Drinks from the living streams of love that roll
By God's high throne. Myriads of glorious ones
Bring their accepted offering. Oh, how blest
To look from this dark prison to that shrine,
To inhale one breath of paradise divine,
And enter into that eternal rest
Which waits the sons of God!"

IF HEAVEN IS what we think it is, and have a right to believe that it is, then the sources of happiness to the saints and angels must be innumerable. The place of the throne of God, the home of angels, and the habitation which our Lord said he would prepare for his disciples is no common country. Heaven is not exhibited to us by precept alone, but by images, symbols, and figures; and it is from these that we are enabled to form our clearest conceptions of the beauty, grandeur, and glory of the place. The richest, most valuable, and most beautiful things that come within the range of our vision while on earth are taken to represent the heaven of heavens. By precept we are taught the fact that there is a heaven, unseen by mortal eye, and by images, symbols, and figures we are taught something of its beauty and glory.

Heaven is represented as a great city, surpassing in magnitude and grandeur anything that mortal eye ever beheld—a city with foundations, walls, and gates composed of the finest and most costly material, the streets of pure gold, and a river of water clear as crystal flowing through the midst of it. The idea of such a city suggests to the mind many things: (1) *Perfect safety.* What enemy could enter such a city? (2) *Unity.* The inhabitants are not strangers and foreigners, but fellow-citizens. They speak one language, are of one heart, one mind, have one Lord and one Father of all—not unison merely, but harmony; not uniformity, but unity, perfect, complete; all moving, talking, and acting under the law of love. (3) *Society.* Social life on earth, imperfect and unsafe as it is, has many pleasures in it, but in the city of God it will be perfect in every particular. No solitaries, no monk's cells, nor dim religious lights will be there. They are all sons of God, and equal heirs with Jesus Christ. (4) *Dignity and beauty.* It is the city of God—the city of the living God. Read the twenty-first and twenty-second chapters of Revelation for a full description. Every citizen a king and priest, and each will feel that he is a citizen of no mean city. Dr. Cummings says, "We shall have the dignity of kings, the sacredness of priests, the sovereignty of a kingdom, the solemnity of a temple; and God himself, our Saviour, shall be the glory in the midst of us. Dignity, then, is inseparable from the idea of such a city. (5) *Permanency.* A city of foundations, "whose builder and maker is God"; the grandeur and beauty of which shall never fade away. The material out of which this city is built is as imperishable as the throne itself. The patriarchs dwelt in tents and tabernacles, but they looked for a city where they might abide. They were willing to be pilgrims and sojourners for a while, but they did not want to be pilgrims forever. The city for which Abraham looked was the one which John saw and described; and it is that same city toward which Christians are looking to-day.

Dr. Guthrie says: "It is a city never built with hands, nor with the years of time; a city whose inhabitants no census has numbered; a city through whose streets rushes no tide of business, nor nodding hearse creeps slowly with its burden to the tomb; a city without griefs or graves, without sins or sorrow, without births or burials, without marriages or mournings; a city which glories in having Jesus for its king, angels for its guards, saints for its citizens; whose walls are salvation, and whose gates are praise."

Far above the reach of our mortal vision this city rises in the imagination with all its grandeur and beauty. O city of the living God, with walls of jasper and gates of pearl! Shall it be my everlasting home? Shall I, with kindred dear, wander along the banks of that beautiful river? Yes, I may, for here are gates on all sides, and they are open all the time, and will be until the very last saint shall have entered. But something whispers to me and says, "You are a great sinner, and nothing unholy shall ever enter that sinless city." "Yes, I know I am a great sinner, — one among the chief of sinners, — but, glory to God and the Lamb, I have a great Saviour, one that is able to save to the uttermost, whose blood cleanseth from all sin. In his *name* I am steering for the city. HOSANNA!"

> "When shall mine eyes thy heaven-built walls
>   And pearly gates behold;
> Thy bulwark with salvation strong,
>   Thy streets of shining gold?"

Another source of happiness will be the environments. Mention of this is made in another chapter, but I wish in this connection to group together a number of facts, so as to get before the mind the combined sources of happiness awaiting the children of God. The saints are to be all immortal and glorified, made in appearance like the glorified humanity of the Redeemer. In this state the whole man will be perfect—the hearing acute, the vision clear, and the mind unencumbered by the weight of frail matter. Heaven, the great central empire of the universe, with its endless variety of beauty and wonders, will be reviewed. New beauties will be continually unfolding to the mind and vision. Imagine heaven to be no larger than the sun; it would then be more than twelve hundred thousand times larger than the earth, and it is hardly just to suppose that the place of God's throne is any less, but rather that it is vastly larger than any of the worlds around it. This is my conception of the magnitude of that better country, that city of the living God.

This country, the home of the angels, the dwelling-place of the Most High through all the eternities, will be studied. What wonders, what beauties will be unfolded to the saints! From every nook and corner, and from every spot some new beauty and wonder will appear. Do you say this is overdrawn? That cannot be. No, I cannot as much as reach the base of the everlasting hills. To me the words of our Saviour are running over with meaning,— "In my Father's house are many mansions,"—suggesting the idea of spaciousness and variety. Is God indifferent to the beautiful? Why, then, give us such glimpses of the beautiful as we now see in the sun, moon, and stars? in the clouds, rainbow, and clear, blue sky? What will it be when the mists are all cleared away, and the saints stand in that Presence before which even the angels veil their faces?

Around the central empire, like islands slumbering in a shoreless ocean, are innumerable worlds and systems, all in plain view to the saints in light. When Sirius was examined by Sir William Herschel with his great telescope, "the whole heavens about it were lit up with the splendor of our sky at sunrise; and when the star fairly entered the field of view, the brightness was so overpowering that the astronomer was forced to protect his eyes with colored glass." It was calculated that this star equaled fourteen such suns as ours; and more recent discoveries have proved that the estimate is quite too low. But Sirius is only one star among many. Thousands of others are scattered through the realms of space, many of them too distant to be viewed by the astronomer's telescope. Now, all these worlds hung out in space will doubtless come within range of the immortal vision. Will it not be a source of infinite pleasure and delight to the saints to become acquainted with the history of these worlds? Will they be indifferent about the mighty works of Him before whose throne they wait? It is not so even now. Did not the psalmist feel impressed with the magnitude of God's works? "When I consider thy heavens, the work of thy fingers, the moon and the stars, which thou hast ordained." "The heavens declare the glory of God; and the firmament sheweth his handywork [sic]." "He hath made his *wonderful* works to be *remembered*." When, and for what purpose were all these worlds created? Are any of them inhabited? If so, with what order of intelligent beings? Are they superior or inferior to man? Ten thousand things connected with the history of these worlds will be exceedingly interesting and delightful to know. Are there not many things about them that we would like to know even now? Is it likely that the saints will suddenly lose all interest in the mighty works of God? Is it not far more reasonable to believe that when the mists are all cleared away, and the saints are where they can know, that they will be a thousandfold more interested and delighted as the wisdom and power of God are unfolded to their understanding? Clinging to his little earth, blinded and bewildered by the awful effects of sin, and in the midst of fog and dust and smoke, what can we know as compared with what there is to be known? Life is short, the conditions unfavorable, so that we shall not even get through with the alphabet until we go hence. But in the city of God, where the conditions are all favorable, and an eternity to be spent, the saints will enter upon a state of progression, onward and upward, forever and ever.

Another source of happiness to the saints will be the unfolding of the glory of God through the person of Jesus Christ. The saints may never see that great eternal Spirit, but they will see manifestations of his glory revealed through the eternal Son. The saints, while on earth, receive "the light of the knowledge of the glory of God in the face of Jesus Christ." So it may be in heaven. Paul says, "The sufferings of this present time are not worthy to be compared with the glory which shall be revealed to us-ward." Jesus said, "I will that they also, whom thou hast given me, be with me where I am; that they may behold my glory." There will be a manifestation of the whole Trinity, such as the saints on earth never witnessed; nor could they endure it in their present condition. When Moses came down from the mount, having been in communion with God, his face shone so brightly that he had to veil it, because the people could not endure it. When Jesus was transfigured on the mount, the disciples who were with him were overpowered by the brightness. But these were only partial manifestations of the glory of God, nothing more than glimpses. What must it be in heaven? The saints, all immortal, will be in a condition not only to endure it, but to enjoy it; for they shall shine like stars and suns. The thought of such coming glory ought to be more than a match for all the ills of this present time.

The glory of God will be revealed not only in what he is in himself, but in what he has done in all the eternities. How little we know about the knowledge, wisdom, power, and goodness of God! When the psalmist mused upon these things he exclaimed, "Such knowledge is too wonderful for me; it is high, I cannot attain unto it." "God's knowledge [that takes in all things, and their reasons, essences, tendencies, and issues] is far beyond me." The saints will see the glory of God not only in creation, to which I have already referred, but in the great and far-reaching plan of human redemption. What elevated and everlasting views the saints will have of the justice and love of God—just in demanding satisfaction for the violation of his law; merciful in providing a sacrifice that could render the satisfaction his justice required. Each saint will realize that if God had not interposed he would not be where he is, nor what he is. How heartily and joyfully they will sing, "Unto him that loved us, …be glory and dominion for ever and ever." There are heights, and depths, and lengths, and breadths in the love of God that the saints on earth know but little about. As these are opened up to the better understanding of the saints in light, it will increase their love and heighten their reverence for the whole Trinity. Turn to that old text, "God so loved the world, that he gave his only begotten Son." Who can explain the full meaning of that little word *so*? An angel could not explain it so that we could comprehend it. It will require all there is of eternity to understand its full meaning.

Another source of happiness will be in a manifestation of the wisdom, goodness, and power of God in his moral government; especially in his providences. The saints will gradually understand, as they did not and could not while on earth, that—

> "God moves in a mysterious way,
> His wonders to perform."

They will also learn that—

The Light of the City *(page 159)*

"And the city had no need of the sun, neither of the moon, to shine in it: for the glory of God did lighten it, and the Lamb is the light thereof" (Rev. 21:23).

"Behind a frowning providence
He hides a smiling face."

They will see in the clearest light how "all things work together for good to them that love God." What they often interpreted as being against them, they will understand was for them. They will understand that God is everywhere, and everywhere at work; that he was here and there about them when they knew it not. Nathaniel was greatly surprised when Jesus told him that he saw him under the fig tree before Philip called to him. Christians do sometimes feel as if they were quite alone in the world, but in heaven they will learn that they were never alone. Ezekiel's vision of the wheels, and the wheel within a wheel, the living creatures, and other complications about the strange vehicle will all be made plain. They will understand how it was, and why it was, that the vehicle and living creatures all moved together, and went *straight* forward and came *straight* back. Jacob carried that dead boy in his heart twenty-two years, and all this time supposed that the vehicle had gone crooked; but when he found Joseph alive and well in Egypt, he saw that the whole affair had gone straight forward. So the saints in heaven learn that while God's ways are above man's ways, they are always and eternally right.

But one of the greatest wonders, and the one in which the saints will see so much glory in God's gracious providences, is the fact that they are saved. Led in ways they had not known, nor would not have chosen, often through gloomy valleys and dark canyons, where scarce a ray of light fell upon their pathway, yet, notwithstanding all this, they are saved, and saved forever. How clear and bright all the ways of God will appear to them in the light of the throne. Tired, weeping, sorrowing one, look up! you are neither alone nor forsaken; God is with you all the time. When Jacob lay down in the evening he felt as though he was quite alone, but when he awoke in the morning he was quite certain that he was not alone. "Surely the Lord is in this place; and I knew it not." So, my beloved, when you stand before the throne, and the wisdom, riches, and glory of God's gracious providences are being unfolded to your understanding, you will realize as never before that he "hath done all things well."

While the saints in heaven will not be as they are on earth, they will not be altogether different. They will retain a personal, conscious existence. Memory will remain; they will not have forgotten their earth. Abraham said to the rich man, "Son, remember." So the saints will remember; and the meeting and recognition of loved ones will be a source of great pleasure and delight. We are not to suppose that the recognition of loved ones will create a spirit of clannishness such as may be found on earth; yet memory, true to her trust, will call up the scenes and relations of earth-life. Love being the supreme law of life in heaven, the saints will not love each other less because of the presence and recognition of those that were near to them on earth. Suppose, when the mists have rolled away (as they surely will), you recognize in the countenance of some one near you a father, mother, brother, sister, or child, it will bring to your consciousness a delight which you could not realize if you did not recognize them. Sitting down with Abraham, Isaac, and Jacob at the banqueting table in heaven, you will not think the less of Abraham because some dear one sits by your side.

Rev. I. L. Kephart, D.D., says: "True companionship will doubtless be a great source of happiness in heaven. To meet there and recognize those with whom we lived, toiled, rejoiced, and wept in this world; to renew acquaintances; to talk over again the experiences of our earth-life—our hopes, fears, joys, sorrows—when once forever saved in heaven; to be with father, mother, brothers, sisters, wife, husband, children, to stroll hand-in-hand on the banks of the River of Life; to talk about and rejoice over the wisdom, goodness, and mercy of our God; to admire and adore the love of Jesus and the great salvation he purchased for us with his own blood—surely, this will be true happiness, this will be heaven."

A Legend.—Death entered a quiet and beautiful home and took from a weeping mother a lovely babe. For many days and months she grieved after the departed one. Twenty years had come and gone when death came again and took the mother. When she entered the heavenly city she saw an innumerable company of white-robed beings, such as she had never looked upon. Presently she saw a little form approaching her, which in a moment she recognized as her departed babe. As they came together the little one said, "Mother, take me in your arms as you used to do." Then she said: "Mother, I have not been sick an hour since I have been here. The angels have taken care of me all the time. They told me you were coming; and when you came in at the gate and they said to me, 'There is your mother,' I knew you at once; and now, dear mother, we are to stay here forever."

Ah, but you say, "That is only a legend." Very true, but it is just such a legend as I love to contemplate, because heaven is just as real as the legend describes it to be. Away with your aerial heaven, your dreamland! Heaven is a place, a real, substantial habitation, a city, a country, a real home, with all the charms that can inhere in our most exalted conceptions of a perfect home. Each saint will retain a personal, conscious individuality. Each will know himself, and know that he is himself.

The worship in heaven will be attended with the most exquisite delight. Everything will be in the most perfect harmony—no discord, no break anywhere. *They all worship.* John gives an idea of the order of heavenly worship. He saw a great company which no man can number millions of millions, from every nation, kingdom, and tribe on earth. They "stood before the throne,... clothed with white robes, and palms in their hands; and cried with a loud voice, saying, Salvation to our God, which sitteth upon the throne, and unto the Lamb." Then he saw the angels which stood about the throne, fall on their faces, saying, "Amen: Blessing, and glory, and wisdom, and thanksgiving, and honour, and power, and might, be unto our God for ever and ever, Amen." That will be a jubilee service worthy the name—a kind of reunion, such as neither saints nor angels ever witnessed. That is *worship*, not a mere performance. Beloved, shall we, some glad, bright day, join with that innumerable host and worship before the throne of the Most High?

Father Almighty, grant it for Jesus' sake.

I cannot do better than give the idea of Dr. Hamilton concerning the nature and order of worship in heaven: "Adoration at the throne, activity in the temple—the worship of the heart, the worship of the voice, the worship of the hands; the whole being consecrated and devoted to God—these are the services of the upper sanctuary. Here the flesh is often wearied with an hour of worship; *there* they rest not day nor night, saying, 'Holy, holy, holy, Lord God Almighty, which was, and is, and is to come.' Here a week will often see us weary in well-doing; there they are drawn on by its own deliciousness to larger and larger fulfillments of Jehovah's will. Here we must lure ourselves to work by the prospect of rest hereafter; there the toil is luxury, and the labor recreation, and nothing but jubilees of praise and holidays of higher service are wanted to diversify the long and industrious Sabbath of the skies. And it matters not that sometimes the celestial citizens are represented as always singing, and sometimes as always resting; for there the work is rest, and every movement, songs; and the many mansions make one temple, and the whole being of its worship one tune—one mighty anthem, long as eternity and large as its burden, the praise of the great

Three-one, the self-renewing and ever-sounding hymn, in which the flight of every seraph, and the harp of every saint, and the smile of every raptured spirit is a several note, and repeat over and over again, 'Holy, holy, holy, Lord God Almighty, which was, and is, and is to come.'" Pilgrim stranger, what do you think of such a country, of such a home? Is it worth an effort to get there? Remember, you must go somewhere soon. You cannot remain here always. Are you journeying toward that better country? Are you sure of it? You cannot afford to make any mistake in a matter of such tremendous importance. Remember that one journey from the cradle to the grave fixes your eternal destiny. Shall it be heaven?

Another source of happiness will be the consciousness that this home will abide; it will stay forever and ever. Long ago one said, "For we are strangers before thee, and sojourners, as were all our fathers: our days on the earth are as a shadow, and there is none abiding." Even though life should be continued fourscore years, it is soon ended, and "we fly away." This is, and has always been the feeling of thoughtful persons. There abides in the human consciousness a sense of unrest, of insecurity. We build and furnish houses and call them homes, but we know they are only temporary, that there is none abiding. The world is one great family of movers, home-seekers. Few persons, except children, live and die where they were born. Oceans, mountains, and continents have been crossed in search of homes, and when they were found they proved to be no more than stopping-places. The Old Testament saints realized this, and hence looked for a city of foundations, a country, a home that would abide. They were tired of living in tents and tabernacles. The sacred Scriptures assure us that there is such a country, such an abiding home, where the inhabitants will stay forever. None will be heard to say, I am weary, or tired, or homesick. Satisfied, forever satisfied!

No feeling of unrest or insecurity will ever enter the minds of the saints in light. Our conceptions of eternity are very feeble and unsatisfactory. We have no word to express it, no word that will convey to our understanding any definite idea of it. Our minds are not strong enough to grasp it. Schoolmen define it, "an ever-abiding present." Theologians define it, "Infinite duration: duration discharged from all limits, without beginning, without succession, and without end." Still we are at sea. Maybe we shall understand it better when the waves of time have ceased to break at our feet. But, define it to be "infinite duration," or duration indefinitely continued. We cannot help but feel that to enter into such a state of bliss, with ever-increasing pleasure and delight, will be indescribably glorious. What more could be desired? All that we can think or speak, and ten thousand times more, is implied and included in an endless life in heaven.

Rev. W. M. Bell, D.D., says: "To my mind, one of the chief sources of happiness to the saints in heaven will be its social fellowship. This happiness, first of all, will consist in the fact that there, for the first time, our eyes shall fall upon the form of our adorable Lord and Saviour. During the years of our earthly pilgrimage we have worshiped and loved our Lord as the unseen Christ; *there* we shall see him as he is. The privilege of reunion and fellowship with those who have gone from us will be the occasion of indescribable happiness. We never quite know how lovely they are, and never fully appreciate them until they are gone. Years of separation shall but serve to make our joy the greater when once again we may greet those from whom we have been separated so long."

Another source of happiness to the saints will be the companionship of angels. Mention is made of this elsewhere, but here I wish to consider it more particularly. Angels are spiritual beings. They are not spirits, as some have supposed, but spiritual. They have visible, tangible forms; beautiful, pure, loving, and lovable. While, in a sense, they may be strangers to the saints, the saints will not be strangers to the angels. They are "ministering spirits sent forth to minister for them who shall be heirs of salvation." And they encamp round about them that fear the Lord, and deliver them. The saints cannot see them now, but they can see the saints, so that they know a great deal about them during their earth-life.

"Millions of spiritual creatures walk the earth,
Unseen, both when we wake, and when we sleep."

They possess superior intelligence. They have never sinned, and "dwell amid the effulgence of heavenly light." For ages unnumbered they have been observing the unfolding of the wisdom, power, and glory of the Creator, and doubtless have been winging their unwearied flight to various and distant parts of God's dominions, to execute the divine command and witness the wonders of the divine administration. We know that once and again they have visited this world, and so, we judge, it is with other parts of the mighty universe.

These pure, intelligent, sympathetic, loving beings are to be the familiar companions of the saints in light, and, for aught we know, will be their instructors in many things. We cannot realize what pleasure it will afford to be associated with them. Oh, how many things they can tell the saints, who with exquisite delight will listen to their recital of what they witnessed long before man was created!

When once the soul has flown away from time and the ever-changing scenes of earth, and passed through the gate into the eternal city, the city of the living God, there will come over it a sense of safety and security which an angel could not describe. While on earth, we go plodding along through sunshine and shadow, through deep, dark ravines, and over rugged mountains, weeping and smiling, hoping and fearing, trusting and doubting, often half-bewildered, wondering when and how this whole matter will end. But, once inside the walls of jasper and gates of pearl, the question will be settled forever and ever. Home at last! victory through the blood of the Lamb! "To him be glory, and honor, and praise, and dominion for ever and ever. Amen."

An honest Christian man, speaking in a testimony meeting, said: "Brethren, I hardly know how this matter will end with me. I sometimes think I will reach heaven at last; and then again I doubt it. I make many mistakes, sometimes stumble and almost fall. I am often half bewildered, and scarcely know which way I am going; but I will struggle on, and if at last the Lord Jesus gets me through safely, *he will never hear the last of it.*"

> "Ear hath not heard the songs
>   Of rapturous praise within that shining portal;
> No heart of man hath dreamed what bliss belongs
>   To that redeemed and joyous blood-washed
>   throng,
>   All glorious and immortal."

XI
HEAVEN — NEGATIVE DESCRIPTIONS

HEAVEN IS PRESENTED to our view in figures, images, and symbols; also in positives and negatives. From these sources, which a kind and merciful Father has provided, we may obtain some glimpses of that spiritual realm. It is safe to presume, however, that the half has not yet been seen or understood. Human language cannot describe it, and we are not in a condition to understand the meaning of heavenly language. Our Lord desired that his disciples should be with him that they might behold his glory. Who on earth comprehends the heavenly meaning of the word *glory?* We attach a meaning to it such as we can understand, but the heavenly meaning is beyond our reach; so with other words, positive and negative, used to describe the heavenly condition of the saints. "After all the discoveries and demonstration of our boasted modern science, we have as much reason as had the friends of Job, three thousand years ago, to exclaim, What can we know?

Paul expressed a desire to depart and be with Christ, which he said was not only better, but *far better.* The patriarchs were looking for a "better country," but who can tell how much better? Who can understand Paul when he speaks of a "far more exceeding and eternal weight of glory"? What do we know about an "eternal weight of glory"? Let our schoolmen, mathematicians, and theologians solve the problem if they can. John says, "It doth not yet appear what we shall be." It is not yet manifest. This much we know, that when Christ shall appear, "we shall be like him." But what is it to be like Christ? When only a glimpse of his glory was revealed to his disciples on the mount it overwhelmed them. Yet we are to be like him—these vile bodies are to be changed and fashioned like unto his glorious body.

Thus far I have given some of the positive, or direct, descriptions of that better country. In this brief chapter I will give some negative descriptions. From these we may be able to form some idea which will be as helpful as any we may gather from the positive side. It is very delightful to know what will be there, and scarcely less delightful to know what will not be there. The Holy Scriptures tell us much of heaven by telling us what it is not:

There is no sin in heaven. —But what do we know about living in a sinless land? We have not had a moment's experience or observation of life in such a country. From the moment we open our eyes to the light until we close them in death, we are in the midst of sin; its dire consequences are all around us and in us. Everything we see or touch is tainted with sin. The food we eat, the water we drink, the air we breathe, the light that falls so lightly upon our pathway, the flowers which bloom around us, are all characterized by imperfection, and are not at all what they would be if it were not for sin. Wars and commotions, earthquakes and famine, with all the physical, mental, and moral distresses seen, heard, and experienced on earth are the fruits of sin. But for this indescribable evil, we could have peace and pleasure all the time. Sin is the Trojan horse that bears with it sword, famine, and pestilence. It is a coal, which not only burns, but blackens. Under its dire influence "every heart has its grief, every house has its skeleton, every character is marred with weakness and imperfection." Do not facts such as these help us to understand how much the Bible means when it teaches plainly and unequivocally that there is no sin in heaven? Nothing unholy or unclean can ever enter the final home of the saints. O sinless clime, O blessed summerland; how delightfully different from earth!—the place itself absolutely pure, every inhabitant pure, every word, thought, and act pure. Who can tell what it will be to live in such a realm?

> "Ear hath not heard the song
>   Of rapturous praise within that shining portal;
> No heart of man hath dreamed what bliss belongs
> To that redeemed and joyous blood-washed
>   throng,
>   All glorious and immortal."

No night shall be in heaven. —This is perhaps one of the most comprehensive and beautiful negative descriptions of heaven ever written or spoken. History, experience, and observation have taught us some lessons concerning night scenes on earth. There is physical, mental, and moral night on earth. We know something of all these, and this will help us to form some conception of a country where there is no night, no literal night. There is no division of time such as we have here, no morning nor evening, no rising nor setting of the sun; "the city hath no need of the sun, neither of the moon, to shine in it: for the glory of God did lighten it, and the Lamb is the light thereof." Think of a whole realm being lighted up by a soft, mellow, and yet brilliant light, proceeding from the throne, falling equally upon every part of the city, and no shadow anywhere. Add to this the fact that saints and angels will shine like stars of the first magnitude. No, no, there will be no night in heaven as long as the throne of God and the Lamb remain. Set this picture over against some night scenes which we have witnessed on earth. The storm king is raging, lightnings flashing, thunders rolling, and the darkness impenetrable—oh, those gloomy, dismal, fearful nights! But there is no night in heaven. Night is not only an emblem of gloom, but of ignorance, sadness, and sorrow. In every earthly home there is some one to suffer, physically or mentally, some face over which the pale shadow of sickness or sorrow has passed. There is no home from which the grim shadow of death can be shut out.

> "Death enters, and there's no defense;
> His time there's none can tell."

Then follow those long, sad nights of waking, when some loved one lies dead in our homes. Such night scenes "wring from every heart the cry of woe"; but, sad as they are, they should "keep alive in our hearts a more intense longing for a home where there shall be no night of sorrow, sadness, or ignorance."

> "No dreadful hour
> Of mental darkness or the tempter's power;
> Across whose skies no envious cloud shall roll
> To dim the sunlight of the soul."

There have been, and still are, night scenes on earth sad enough to move the stoutest hearts and enlist the sympathy of angels. Look at the field of battle, the night following a day of hard fighting, when hundreds of dead and wounded lie side by side. See that ship in mid-ocean, the night dark as darkness itself; the storm raging, the vessel wrecked and drifting, with hundreds of men, women, and children clinging to each other, with nothing before them but a grave in the deep blue sea. See that mother at the midnight hour bending over the cradle, watching the last moments of her dying babe. Such night scenes on earth are continually repeating themselves, and will continue until the consummation of all earthly things. Is not the possibility, yea, the hope of living in a land where there is no night infinitely more inspiring than the cold, cheerless thought of annihilation?

> "No night shall be in heaven; no gathering gloom
> Shall o'er that glorious landscape ever come;
> No tears shall fall in sadness o'er those flowers
> That breathe their fragrance through celestial bowers.
> No night shall be in heaven; no darkness roam,
> No bed of death, no silence of the tomb;
> But breezes ever fresh with love and truth
> Shall brace the frame of an immortal youth."

No death shall be in heaven. — This is good news from a far country. We know "it is appointed unto men once to die," and there is no escape, no discharge in this war; but there is a country where the inhabitants never die, never grow old, are never weary, never sick, and never sad. Death reigns here, and we must meet it. However familiar we may seem to be with death, there is a deep and inexplicable mystery about it. If we knew what life is, we might form some better conception of death; but, not knowing the former, we cannot fully comprehend the latter. We know what some of the effects of death are from the earth side, but that is not death itself. Schoolmen, scientists, and theologians have tried to define death, but have never succeeded even to their own satisfaction. Whatever may be the physical suffering in approaching the end, death in itself is as painless as falling asleep. But whatever opinion we may form of death, there is something about it that all thoughtful persons would escape if they could. The wisest and best of earth have a sacred dread of passing through the valley of the shadow of death. The Christian is cheered and comforted by the hope of something better beyond, but if he had the opportunity of reaching that goodly land without dying he would doubtless accept it.

Death has made sad havoc in the world. The number of the slain is many times more than that of the living, and the conquest still goes on. He is no respecter of persons, he enters the palaces of kings the same as the hovels of the poor. The high, the low, the rich, and the poor must bow to his scepter. There is not a day, nor an hour, nor a moment, but the voice of lamentation and weeping may be heard — Rachel weeping for her children because they are not. This is a dying world. Everything in the vegetable and animal world dies — man "dieth and wasteth away." The beasts, birds, insects, and fishes die, the brightest flowers fade and fall. But it is not thus in heaven. Death will never .pass through those gates of pearl, nor see inside those jasper walls. Oh heaven, land of the living, land of immortal youth and fadeless beauty where the voice of lamentation and weeping over the dead will never be heard! Never, no never! What do we poor mortals, walking among the dying and the dead, know about living in such a land, where the loved ones at our side will stay forever? We have the theory, the promise, and the hope, but "what must it be to be there?" If there were such a land on earth, how the living would flock to it, and but few would leave it for the sake of dying. But earth has no such an oasis; no green spot where the people live forever. Death reigns everywhere. "And all the days of Methuselah were nine hundred sixty and nine years; and he died." That was the sequel — "and he died." "We must needs die," for so it is written — written in the Book; written in our hearts; written on our foreheads; written all about us. In a sense, it is "paying the debt of nature." To a skeptic that is all it means, but to a

Christian it means something more; yes, a great deal more. J. Foster says, "It is rather like bringing a note to a bank to obtain solid gold in exchange for it. In this case you bring this cumbrous body which is worth nothing, and which you could not wish to retain long; you lay it down and receive for it from the eternal treasures, liberty, victory, knowledge, and rapture."

In that better country all the penal consequences of sin will be unfelt and unknown. Weariness, anxiety, pain, toil, sorrow, want, disappointment, temptation, fear, hunger, thirst, and weeping will be unknown. These are among the things which will not be there. What do we or can we know about living in the absence of all these ills? The soul, washed in the blood of the Lamb, will be as pure as if it had never been stained with sin, so that from within and without all will be pure, peaceful, restful, and delightful. But lest some one might think this is overdrawn, we turn to the Bible. Thank God for this sure word of prophecy! Theories may fail, imagination may overdraw, but the Word of the Lord shall stand. Here is solid rock, upon which we may plant our feet and smile amid "the wrecks of matter and the crash of worlds." Hallelujah! Turning to this sacred volume, we read, "And the ransomed of the Lord shall return, and come to Zion with songs and everlasting joy upon their heads: they shall obtain joy and gladness, and sorrow and sighing shall flee away." "These are they which came out of great tribulation, and have washed their robes, and made them white in the blood of the Lamb. . . . They shall hunger no more, neither thirst any more; neither shall the sun light on them, nor any heat. For the Lamb which is in the midst of the throne shall feed them, and shall lead them unto living fountains of waters: and God shall wipe away all tears from their eyes." "And I heard a great voice out of heaven saying, Behold, the tabernacle of God is with men, and he will dwell with them, ...and be their God. And God shall wipe away all tears from their eyes; and there shall be no more death, neither sorrow, nor crying, neither shall there be any more pain: for the former things are passed away." "And I saw as it were a sea of glass mingled with fire: and them that had gotten the victory... stand on the sea of glass, having the harps of God. And they sing the song of Moses the servant of God, and the song of the Lamb, saying, Great and marvellous are thy works, Lord God Almighty; just and true are thy ways, thou King of saints." Could human imagination in her most lucid moments ever paint a more beautiful and desirable picture of heaven than these sacred writers have done? In such a place, with such environments, the saints of God are to dwell forever and ever.

> "There shall they muse amid the starry glow,
> Or hear the fiery streams of glory flow;
> Or, on the living cars of lightnings driven,
> Triumphant, whirled around the plains of heaven."

I wish, in closing this chapter, to emphasize this thought, that the chief joy and delight of the saints will be the immediate, personal, and visible presence of Jesus Christ in all his glory. Here, in this time-haze, we follow him by faith. Often with doubts and fears we plod along, scarcely knowing which way we are going. Temptations, losses, crosses, and many other ills overtake us in the pilgrimage of life. Faith is often beclouded with inexplicable providences, so that scarce a ray of light falls upon our pathway. In these dark hours the heart cries out, "Oh that I knew where I might find him!" But in heaven it will not be thus. "We shall see him as he is," "face to face." We shall see him in the glory and majesty both of the divine and human nature. We shall hear his voice, see his hands that were wounded, and his brow that was pierced with thorns. Paul knew a great deal about Christ, for he had seen him, and at one time expressed a desire to depart and be with him, which he says is far better. His highest ideal of heaven and heavenly bliss was to be like Christ and be with him. Can anything be more inspiring and uplifting to the human soul than what John saw? "The Lamb which is in the midst of the throne shall feed them, and shall lead them unto living fountains of waters." The thought of being in that innumerable company, with bodies fashioned like unto his glorious body, ought to enliven our faith, hope, and love, and quicken our steps homeward. It is no dream, no hallucination, but a grand, glorious fact that "the saints of the Most High shall take the kingdom and possess the kingdom for ever, *even for ever and ever.*"

A little negro boy, when near to death, expressed the desire to depart and be with Christ. "But," said some one standing by, "suppose Jesus should leave heaven, what would you then do?" He replied, "I would follow him wherever he went." "But suppose he should go to hell, what would you do?" "Ah, massa," he quickly replied, "there is no hell where Jesus is."

> "Who, trusting in their Lord, depart,
> Cleansed from all sin, and pure in heart;
> The bliss unmixed, the glorious prize
> They find with Christ in paradise.
> Yet, glorified by grace alone,
> They cast their crowns before the throne,
> And fill the echoing courts above
> With praises of redeeming love."

XII
HEAVEN — PREPARATIONS FOR

"But oh! I am told in God's blessed Word
That transgressions must all be forgiven;
That sin must be vanquished and passion sub
    dued,
Ere my soul sees the mansions of heaven."

LONG AGO A VOICE came ringing down from heaven: "Prepare to meet thy God." Later, the greatest teacher the world ever knew said, "Be ye also ready: for in such an hour as ye think not the Son of man cometh." When the children of Israel were about to cross the river Jordan and enter the land of promise, Joshua said to the people, "Sanctify yourselves: for to-morrow the Lord will do wonders among you." For *"ye have not passed this way heretofore."* They had been wandering around in the wilderness for a long time, and had seen and experienced much of the wisdom, power, and goodness of God. But now a new experience confronted them; they were to cross the river which divided the wilderness and their long-wished-for promised land. This to them was the event of their lives, not only the fact itself, but the manner of its accomplishment. "After all we have seen and heard, shall we in very fact enter the land of Canaan to-morrow?" This was no ordinary affair to them. They had heard their fathers and mothers tell how they had crossed the Red Sea, and now they were to cross the river. How their hearts must have throbbed with emotion. Joshua felt the importance of it, for he said, "To-morrow the Lord will do wonders among you."

In view of what was just before them, he said, "Sanctify yourselves." 'Whatever opinions we may have concerning the exact meaning of the word *sanctify,* as it occurs in this place, one thing is certain, that it cannot mean less than *preparation.* Wash yourselves, cleanse your garments, and abstain from everything that might indispose your minds from a proper and profitable attention to the miracle about to be wrought in your behalf. But it was a literal river they were about to cross, and a literal Canaan they were about to enter. Sin was on both sides of the river. If such a preparation as Joshua commanded was necessary for such an event, what preparation will be necessary to go from an earthly to a spiritual realm—from a land of sin and death to a place of absolute purity? While the Canaan side in many respects was better than the wilderness side, yet it was under the curse, and was full of sin, sorrow, misery, and death. Not so with that "better country" toward which the patriarchs looked. Sin, with all its evil consequences, reigns over all the earth, but *there* is *no sin in heaven.*

Peter, when speaking of the consummation of all earthly affairs,—when the heavens shall pass away, the elements melt with fervent heat, and the earth, with all its works, shall be burned up,—asked this solemn and far-reaching question, "What manner of persons ought ye to be in all holy conversation and godliness?" How careful and thoughtful we ought to be in answering this question. We cannot afford to make any mistake. Eternal things inhere in it. Brushing aside all theories and all speculations, we turn to the Holy Scriptures for an answer. Let us make it personal. *"What manner of person ought I to be to go from earth to heaven?* "Blessed are the pure in heart: for they shall see [possess] God." "Be ye therefore perfect, as your Father which is in heaven is perfect." "Follow peace with all men, and holiness, without which no man shall see the Lord." "And there shall in no wise enter into it [the city] any thing that defileth, neither whatsoever worketh abomination, or maketh a lie: but they which are written in the Lamb's book of life." "If we confess our sins, he is faithful and just to forgive us our sins, and to cleanse us from all unrighteousness." "The blood of Jesus Christ his Son cleanseth us from all sin." "They [the saints] have washed their robes, and made them white in the blood of the Lamb." From these and many other similar passages we learn: (1) That heaven is a place of absolute holiness; that neither sin nor any impurity can ever enter there. (2) That a state of holiness or perfection is attainable in this life, and is an unconditional prerequisite to entering heaven. (3) That ample provisions have been made for our purification — "The blood of Jesus Christ his Son cleanseth us from all sin," "and from all unrighteousness." He is able to save to the uttermost.

Men may reason, argue, and dispute on the doctrine of sanctification, holiness, and perfection in its relation to man while on earth; they may ransack creation to find definitions and analogies to modify these terms, but these facts remain and will remain forever: (1) God is holy. (2) Heaven is holy. (3) Man must be holy to dwell with God. Dr. Newman says: "Holiness, or inward separation from the world, is necessary to our admission into heaven, because heaven is not a place of happiness — except to be holy... God cannot change his nature. Holy he must ever be. But while he is holy, no unholy soul can be happy in heaven."

But some men seem to be expecting too much in death or in the resurrection; that in some way or other they will be fitted for heaven in one, or the other, or both these events. But neither death nor the resurrection has anything to do with the moral nature in man—they both relate to the physical or outer man. The foolish virgins fell asleep without oil in their vessels, and when they awoke their vessels were empty still. "If a tree fall toward the south, or toward the north, in the place where the tree falleth, there shall it be." "Whatsoever a man soweth, that shall he also reap." We sow in time, and reap in eternity. A fitness for heaven implies many things; not only moral purity in the abstract, but whatever flows from a pure fountain—love, peace, gentleness, kindness, sympathy, and joy. All these graces or excellencies are to be secured in this life. They all inhere in the life and character of a genuine Christian, for they all belong to Christ, and Paul says, "Ye are complete in him." Suppose we stop a moment and take an inventory of what we have in Christ: (1) We may be "partakers of the divine nature." (2) The Christ-life within. "I live; yet not I, but Christ liveth in me." (3) "But we have the mind of Christ." (4) "The spirit of Christ." Show me a man, rich or poor, white or black, learned or unlearned, that has the nature, life, mind, and spirit of Christ and I will show you a genuine Christian. These, with what combines in them, is what the apostle calls *completeness in Christ.* They will constitute a complete fitness for heaven, and may all be secured here and now. Better stop wrangling over the meaning of words and by a mighty act of faith and consecration press into a higher chamber of Christian experience, and be "filled with all the fulness of God."

Heaven is a holy place for holy inhabitants, a prepared place for a prepared people. A soul, all polluted with sin, if carried into the midst of heaven, would be miserable. Holiness alone, with what inheres in it and flows from it, is the one only valid qualification for entering heaven. Less than this will not suffice. Beloved, what is your present experience? What are your thoughts concerning the life to come? Does the anticipation of an endless home with the pure and good inspire you to greater activity? Paul said: "I press toward the mark for the prize." "I count all things but loss... that I may win Christ." Are you willing to press, toil, and make sacrifices as you journey toward that better country? Are you trying to persuade others to go with you? Is the hope of being with Christ, the angels, and your loved ones more than a match for the losses you sustain and the crosses you bear? When Paul reached the end of his eventful life he reviewed the past, considered the present, and turning to the future, said, "I am now ready... and the time of my departure is at hand." His had been a busy life. He had gone here and there, laboring, toiling, and suffering to build up and extend the kingdom of the Christ whom he loved so well, and with whom he expected to live forever.

But now a new experience confronted him. He must die; not "in the chamber where the good man meets his fate," but at the martyr's block. Nevertheless he said, "I am now ready." Then he assigned three reasons why he was ready: (l) "I have fought a good fight." He had not only fought bravely and skillfully, but he had fought in a good cause. On land and sea, at home and abroad, among friends and foes, he had stood for the right. (2) "I have finished my course." Once before he had expressed the desire to depart and be with Christ, but he was not ready, because his work was not yet done. But now he was ready; he had finished his course, had done all the Master had for him to do. (3) "I have kept the faith." He had the utmost confidence in the authenticity and inspiration of Old Testament Scriptures. In his public discourses, as well as in his epistles, he quoted from them freely; and you cannot read a doubt into anything he said or wrote. He did not seem to know anything about modern "higher criticism." And from the time of his conversion at Damascus to the day when he laid his head on the block he never gave place for a doubt concerning the Messiahship of Jesus Christ. He believed and taught all the fundamental doctrines of Christ's religion. He not only understood the theory of Christianity, but he had a personal, conscious experience which he always kept well in the forefront. He knew a man in Christ. He knew that the gospel was the power of God unto salvation to all that believed. He knew that a penitent soul was justified by faith, and had peace with God. He knew there was no condemnation to them that were in Christ. He knew that the Spirit of Christ here witnessed with his spirit that he was a child of God. He knew that God sent forth the Spirit of his Son into his own heart "crying, Abba, Father." He knew that a Christian stood, lived, and walked by faith. All these things Paul had kept, and when the end came he said, "I am now ready"—ready to depart and be with Christ. We are not required to do in every respect just *what* Paul did, but if we would be ready as he was ready we must do *as* he did—fight a good fight, finish our course, and keep the faith, which, if we do, we shall be crowned as certainly as he was.

We do not know just where we are in the voyage of life. Some are in mid-ocean, while others are near the shore; but wherever we are we should carefully take our bearings, so as to know beyond a peradventure which way we are drifting. There are two ports beyond, into one of which we shall enter soon. If we are heirs of God, and joint-heirs with Jesus Christ, we shall enter the harbor of bliss and be forever at home with the pure and good.

> "Hark! it is the bridegroom's voice
> Welcome, pilgrim, to thy rest!
> Now, within the gate rejoice,
> Safe, and sealed, and bought, and blessed."

Concluding Thoughts

I have given in this little book a few glimpses of that better country, but they are only glimpses. Other thoughts came, but they were too agile for me, I could not hold them long enough to find words to express them. Imagination often finds herself bewildered, and loses what she seemed to have. Whoever undertakes to describe heaven and the heavenly condition of the saints in light will find himself in an ocean of thoughts without words to express them. Who can imagine the beauty and grandeur of a place prepared by the King of saints? Who can describe a city such as John saw? Who can describe a country, the inhabitants of which shine like the stars and the whole realm lit up by a light proceeding from the throne. The queen of Sheba had heard of the wisdom of Solomon, the beauty of the temple and the grandeur of his surroundings while yet in her own country, but when she came and saw it, it so far exceeded all she had heard and all she could imagine that she said the half had not been told her. So it will be when the saints are all gathered home. They shall see the King in his beauty, the glory of his kingdom, and each will realize that the half had not been told.

I am now near the base of life's rugged mountain, on the western slope. I cannot go back if I would. There are only a few steps between me and the river. I know it must be so, for the shadows of life's evening tree are falling thick around me. What if this were all? What if nothing remained for me but the few steps before me, then to cease to be, the same as if I had not been at all? Wherein lies the difference between not beginning to be and ceasing to be? The evening time of life to one who has nothing to look for beyond must be dim and shadowy. But there is something after this life. "In the twilight of a summer's evening a pastor called at the residence of one of his parishioners, and found seated in the doorway a little boy with both hands extended upward, holding to a line. 'What are you doing here, my little friend?' inquired the minister. 'Flying my kite, sir,' was the reply. 'Flying your kite!' exclaimed the pastor; 'I can see no kite; you can see none.' 'I know it, sir,' responded the lad. 'I cannot see it; but I *know* it is there, for I *feel it pull.*'"

We cannot see beyond the river, but if our affections are set on things above we shall realize beyond a peradventure that there is something there for us. All this longing, hoping, and dreaming means something. It cannot all be false. What does it mean? Plutarch, unaided by the light of revelation, but following his own intuitions, said, "I would suppose God to be meanly and idly employed in concerning himself so much about us if we had nothing divine within, or which resembleth his own perfections, nothing that is stable and firm, but were only like leaves, which Homer says wither and fall in a short time. It is absurd to imagine that souls are made only to blossom and flourish for a day in a tender and delicate body of flesh and then be extinguished on every slight occasion." The voice of all the peoples of the earth, from the remotest antiquity, learned and unlearned, high and low, wise and unwise, poets and philosophers, is, that there is something remaining for man after this life. This universal consent is confirmed by a revelation from God, which not only teaches the fact, but points the way leading to an immortal inheritance that fadeth not away.

> "The more our spirits are enlarged on earth,
> The deeper draughts they shall receive of heaven."

Members of Schmul's Wesleyan Book Club buy these outstanding books at 40% off the retail price.

Join Schmul's Wesleyan Book Club by calling toll-free:
800-S$_7$P$_7$B$_2$O$_6$O$_6$K$_5$S$_7$
Put a discount Christian bookstore in your own mailbox.

Visit us on the Internet at
www.wesleyanbooks.com

You may also order direct from the publisher by writing:
**Schmul Publishing Company
PO Box 776
Nicholasville, KY 40340**

www.ingramcontent.com/pod-product-compliance
Lightning Source LLC
Chambersburg PA
CBHW060529100426
42743CB00009B/1467